The Book of Dan

Seventy-nine Years To Redemption

Dan A. Myers, M.D.

Other books by Dan Myers:

<u>Golden Rules for Parenting,</u>
<u>A Child Psychiatrist Discovers the Bible</u>

<u>Biblical Parenting,</u>
<u>A Child Psychiatrist's View</u>

<u>Biblical Parenting,</u>
<u>Chinese Christian Edition</u>

Scripture quotations are from
The New International Bible
Zondervan, 2011

Dan A. Myers, MD - dcabin@gmail.com

Dan Allen Myers

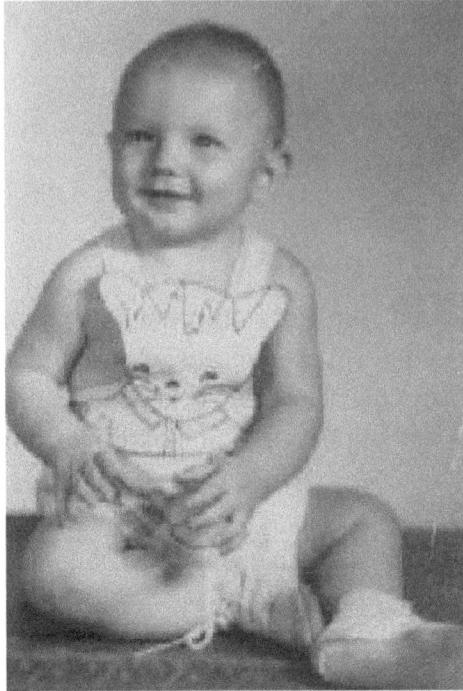

Born with a
"glass half-full"
nature.

Endowed competitive with leadership attributes.

Dedicated To My Grandchildren:
Danielle Howell
Barret Howell
Rock Linton
Boone Howell
Margot Linton
Dylan Thompson
Katie Myers
Kathleen Roberts
Ella Myers
Sarah Roberts
Gretchen Schultz
Annie Myers
Courtney Schultz

Contents

Introduction	8
Childhood	9
Born to Be a Doctor	10
Football	18
Reflections On Childhood	20
Rules for Successful Child Rearing	22
College Age	25
Mexico	31
Mexican Gunslinger	40
Boredom	42
Camp	45
Visitors to the Hacienda	49
Reflection On Mexico Experience	51
Playing Football for Darrell Royal	53
Turn One - Infectious Hepatitis	53
Turn Two - Baylor Med. School	54
Medical Student and Marriage	56
Internship	61
Medical Corps, US Army	63
Administrative Leave	70
Psychiatry Residency	73
Reflections - College Age Period	87
Young Adult Stage	89
Gambling	97
More Real Estate Maneuvering	101
Divorce and The Log Cabin	103
The Manic Alcoholic/Olympics	107
Timeline	114
Remarrying	115
Becoming a Church Guy	122
First Mission Trip - Cuba	124
Reflections on Cuba Trip	131
Second Mission Trip - Romania	137
Reflection on Romania	144
Being Called to China?	146

Reflections on China   163
Flunking Retirement   164
Golf   164
Pecan Valley   165
God Has Other Plans for Me   167
God's Hand   168
Rushing To Redemption   171
Introduction   172
Intelligent Design   173
Evolution   174
Getting Ready For Heaven   175
Is Jesus God?   176
Is the Bible the Word of God?   177
When Reading the Bible
     Doesn't Help   178
When Christianity Seems Unfair   179
When Pride Gets In The Way   180
Unfair Death and Suffering   180
Emergency Salvation   181
Living a Christian Life   182
Alcohol   182
The Bottom Line   185
Reading Suggestions   186

Introduction

The Book of Dan began as a memoir intended only for family and close friends. As the writing progressed I became aware that progress toward redemption was an important theme in my life story.

Religion and Bible study comes relatively late in the memoir. It began seven years after the end of a twenty year marriage to my first wife, Yvonne Brown. I was 47 years old when Kathy Hawn and I married. Before then I would have said I was a Christian, but I did not attend Church, had not read the Bible, and did not live by Christian principles.

This change was not consciously sought or even recognized. Hedonism as a young man was intoxicating but blinding. Godlessness that was perceived as exciting and fun in my youth, in retrospect, seems much more dangerous than I appreciated.

Writing this memoir so opened my eyes to how God had protected and directed my life, I wondered if my story might benefit others struggling with redemptive issues.

Having grown up with minimal Christian influence, memories of my secular childhood, college age, and young adulthood are compared with a Christian mentality. A fifty year career as a child psychiatrist hopefully sharpened rather than warped these perceptions and conclusions.

The initial plan is to give this book to family and friends who would have an interest in the memoir portion. Should the reader know others who might benefit from the redemptive message, they should be referred to amazon.com. Profits from sales will be donated to charity. An established publisher will be sought if Amazon sales indicate a demand.

CS Lewis in The Joyful Christian said, "Aim at Heaven and you will get Earth 'thrown in': aim at Earth and you will get neither." I have been trying but it is easier said than done. At 79 years old I have begun rushing for redemption.

Childhood

(From birth until leaving home for college or work)

Born To Be A Doctor

The year was 1921. A cold and windy morning in the small west Texas town of Cross Plains, Texas. Seven-year-old Cornelius Robertson (C.R.) Myers lay dying of meningitis.

Kneeling at his bedside was my grandmother, Willa Fuller Myers, known as "Mom" by her grandchildren. Willa was praying C.R. would live. Willa had grown up idolizing her physician father, Dr. William Fuller, a respected Dallas physician. Mom regularly told me that being a doctor was a nobler calling than the ministry. She would say that it was physicians, not priests, who shouldn't marry. Mom, a feminist before her time, resented being a woman in Texas in the 1920's as it kept her from becoming a physician.

Desperate for her son to survive, she began to bargain with God. "God, if you let my son live, I will see that he becomes a doctor!" she prayed. C.R. recovered from what in those days was usually a death sentence, spinal meningitis.

Sixteen years later during the Great Depression, my father, C.R. Myers, felt fortunate to be working for Exxon as a roughneck in Talco, Texas. CR would never be a physician. He became a contractor and developer.

On January 14th, 1937 when my mother, Geraldine Beitle Myers, gave birth to me, my grandmother "Mom" was certain I was the one to fulfill her promise to God. I was born to be a doctor, and my grandmother made sure I knew it. In May of 1962, I graduated from Baylor College of Medicine with my grandmother at my side.

My father had been named after his father, Cornelius Robinson Myers, a Katy Railroad train conductor. This grandfather, my namesake, was known by the name, "Dan," because he was such a dandy dresser, a personality trait that obviously is not genetically transmitted. My father was called "Rosy," a nickname acquired from the color he turned when angry, which he often was.

Rosy was a large, muscular man. He left home in the 11th grade to play football at The Schreiner Institute in Kerrville, Texas. A personality profile of Rosy may be best described by the following story:

In his 50's, some golfing buddies gave Rosy a plaque depicting a large troll with a club. The caption read, "Yea, though I walk through the valley of the shadow of death I shall fear no evil."… "Because I am the toughest son-of–a bitch in the valley."

Our mother, Jeri Myers, grew up like a princess in Kerrville, Texas, the daughter of Ally and Freddie Beitel, wealthy owners of a lumberyard. However, during the depression Ally made unsecured loans and lost the lumberyard and his wealth. Jeri was a beauty and Rosy was determined to rescue her from the family's economic crisis. After they married, Rosy struggled to make Jeri's life as "perfect" as the one she had lost. In the process he effectively kept her helpless. Jeri played tennis, bridge and was a playmate to her children. Jeri lived to be a 100 years old, still dressing like a younger woman and having the enthusiasm of a teenager. She was always a fun person. Her grandchildren loved her. She never said an unkind thing about anyone and looked for the positives in her life. My younger sisters, Nancy and Fritzi disgustingly say my mother referred to me as "The Son That Shines." My father's nickname for me was "Knot-Head." As you might guess, I was closer to my mother.

Rosy used to tell the following story about my birth: My parents were living in the oil patch town of Talco, 30 miles from Paris, Texas. There was no hospital in Talco, so Rosy took Jeri to the hospital in Paris, Texas when she was in the early stage of labor. My father returned to Talco expecting to be called by the doctor when the birth was closer at hand. The next day, after the end of a hard day's roughneck work, the doctor called. Rosy got into his new truck and began the 30-mile trip in a snowstorm. On the way he came across a man standing near a car stuck in the snow, waving for him to stop. Rosy stopped, rolled down the window explained the situation about his wife and told the man he would take him into town. The man said the had a chain in his trunk and he would attach it to my dad's rear bumper. If Rosy would give him a pull, he would not even have to get out of his truck. The man attached the chain but after a short pull, Rosy heard and felt what he thought was the chain coming loose. The man knocked on the window, thanked Rosy for his kindness but told him to hurry on to the hospital and he would hail another car Rosy left him there and proceeded to the hospital, arriving in time for my birth. The next morning Rosy decided to try to make it back to Talco. He went to get into his truck and discovered his back bumper was gone!

Jeri was a stay-at-home mom, but she didn't stay at home a lot. My sister Nancy, one and a half years younger, and I enjoyed considerable independence. When Jeri wasn't home, Nancy's direction and protection was assumed by me. Our sister Fritzi, was 10 years younger so she was eight when I left for college, then medical school. Fritzi largely escaped being "parented" by Dan. You would think that would be good. However, after Nancy went off to college, things must have deteriorated at our home. Fritzi remembers a rather traumatic childhood, rife with marital discord, alcohol abuse, and turmoil.

When I was six years old we were living in another oil field town, Hawkins, Texas. An older neighborhood boy had been bullying me. Rosy, disgusted with my coming home crying, told me the next time the boy bothered me, to pick up something and hit him with it. Being more afraid of Rosy than my friend, I intended to obey. Several days later bullying resumed. It occurred in our garage, and the first object I found was a hatchet. Seeing my resolve, the boy took off running toward his house with me fast behind waving the hatchet. When we reached his porch the door was locked so he couldn't get into the house. He turned, managed to take the hatchet from me and whopped me on the head. Fortunately, it was the blunt, not the sharp end, that made contact. we were were still struggling when his mother was able to separate us. It is apparent to me now, the blow caused a depressed skull fracture (since a dent can still be seen on my bald head). Evidently at the time it presented as a swelling or knot, hence the origin of Rosy's nickname for me, "Knot-Head."

As a physician I realize I was fortunate (blessed?) to have no neurologic long term consequences from an undiagnosed and untreated compressed skull fracture. God was looking out for me?

Having Rosy push me to aggressively respond to any perceived attempt of intimidation may have shaped a personality trait that was carried from early childhood to the present. Being beaten at anything became intolerable. Competitiveness became a pervasive aspect of my personality. This, coupled with an underlying fear of my father, yet intensely wanting to please him, resulted in my being exceptionally coachable, aggressive, and competitive in sports. I was tailor-made for playing American football. Sadly the same traits have caused me to be hopeless in whipping golf.

A more serious brush with death occurred from a dove hunting incident as a thirteen year old boy. Walking down a path, with a loaded, bolt-action 410 shotgun, I stepped on a six foot long black rat snake.

Startled, I jumped back shooting the snake from the hip rather than shouldering the gun. The snake was hit mid section but the top half was very much alive. In my excitement I chambered a fresh 410 shell. Rather than shooting the snake again, I hit him in the head with the butt of the shotgun. The shotgun discharged with the barrel pointing directly at my face. It sounded as if it had gone off next to my right ear. A guardian angel?

Growing up, there was little overt religious instruction provided in our family. We attended Church on the major holidays but no saying of grace at meals or references to the Bible. Rosy was a strict disciplinarian, having no tolerance for parental disrespect. Although he didn't quote the Bible, he certainly practiced, "Honor your mother and father." This resulted in my sisters and I being ingrained to respect authority. As an adult practicing child psychiatry, I concluded that failure of parents to teach their children to respect authority was the greatest impediment to children living a long and good life.

By 1944, Rosy had been promoted into an executive position with Exxon and we were living in Houston. Office work didn't suit him so he left Exxon and moved to Waco to start a construction company.

On Monday, December 30, 1946, we had been living in Waco two years. On that day the first of the only two times I remember praying before my second marriage occurred. To be more specific, I actually led a group in prayer at the age of eight. You might think the occasion foreboded a future as a minister?

The temperature that day in Waco was below freezing. My sister, Nancy, age seven, and I each had a friend over that day, and we were all sitting on the floor around the living room radio listening to a weather forecast. We were all excited because a few flakes of snow had stuck on our clothing before we came in from out of the cold. The cold wind howled and shook the sweating large paned windows in the older house Rosy had rented on Dyer Street. The four of us listened intently as the weatherman forecasted continued cold and wind with scattered snow flurries but no accumulation.

There were moans and groans as we lamented having our hope for a snowy winter playground dashed. From God knows where the idea came, I said, "Let us pray for snow." We held hands and I prayed, "Please! Please! God make it snow a lot." and we all said, "Amen." The next morning we awakened to the stillness of the wind and the bright light reflected by a blanket of fallen snow. Tuesday, December 31, 1946 Waco, Texas had recorded the largest snowfall in its history.

Even as a eight year old, my soul seems defended from understanding God's importance in my life. My remembrance of this childhood miracle is void of any credit given to a Heavenly Father or recognition that prayer could be an asset in the future. I treated it as if I had wished on a rabbit's foot or dismissed it as a coincidence.

From an early age, my summers were spent working for Rosy's construction company. Initially he had me cleaning the job sites, and working as a carpenter's helper. Getting older and stronger resulted in carrying shingles up ladders to roofers, spreading and tamping fresh concrete, and unloading trucks. In those times no colleges or high school programs had discovered the benefit of weight training. Working for Rosy Myers Construction Company was a fortunate substitute.

One summer Rosy had a job in McGregor, Texas, about 20 miles from Waco. My friend Tommy Flood was also working in McGregor but on a different shift. We would pass each other as we came back and forth to Waco. To enhance the excitement of the boring trip, we would play chicken when we met on the highway, seeing which one of us would yield to the other's car.

Once, Rosy's car was in the shop so he took my car and Tommy ran him off the road thinking it was me. Rosy came home that night steaming mad. He asked, "What's wrong with that crazy son of a bitch?" I told him I didn't know. Later Tommy called to tell me he was impressed that I stuck it out longer than usual before backing down and leaving the road. When he heard it was Rosy rather than me in the car, you could hear a pin drop. Tommy stayed clear of our house for a while and it put a damper on any romantic interest in my sister, Nancy. Was it just luck that Tommy and I didn't kill each other?

My parents let me attend Camp Stewart in the Texas Hill Country when I was thirteen. Waiting tables paid one half of my tuition. My girl friend, Barbara, was going to be at Camp Waldemar and they had dances with Camp Stewart. It didn't work out the way it was planned. All dances were cancelled that summer because of a polio epidemic. However that camp experience paid other dividends. Later in my life, my experience at Camp Stewart served as a model for developing the program for a boy's camp in the state of Tamaulipas, Mexico.

During Junior High School, I got better at pleasing adults, became competitive in academics, improved my athleticism by playing football, basketball, and running track. Staying free from serious sport injuries has been a great blessing.

My only broken bone was of my right arm sustained during Junior High spring football training. Dr. Wilson Crosthwait, a Waco doctor who would influence other aspects of my life course, put on the cast. When the swelling in my arm lessened I found that if I poured talcum powder into the space between my arm and the cast to stop the itching when I moved my arm slightly it would emit a puff of white powder. It was fun doing this when some girl was signing my cast.

During Junior High I developed a strong interest in reading adventure novels, particularly the classics and historical fiction. This was a source of considerable irritation to Rosy who would get on me for always having my nose in a book.

In high school I was one of a few freshman who made the varsity football team. Being of average size, speed and skill, my gifts were physical stamina, competitiveness, a high pain threshold, and that I took coaching exceptionally well (respect for authority and wanting to please.) Known as a "hitter" I sustained, and undoubtably gave, unrecognized concussions. There were college games where I played an entire half without remembering what happened. Playing hurt was an asset. Coaches liked to have me around as an example. As a senior at Waco High I was a class 5A all state selection at end for both offense and defense which made me a blue chip recruit. Rosy's comment to my discussing the dilemma about which program to select was, "If you are waiting for me to feel sorry for you, you are going to have to change the subject." I eventually decided to accept a University of Texas scholarship.

In the summer of 1955 I was at Boy's State, elected governor, and was made honorary "Governor of Texas" for a day. Several proclamations on that day were signed, Dan Myers, Acting Governor of the State of Texas.

Lt. Gov. Ed Bourg   Gov. Dan Myers

I graduated 4th in my senior high school class and was admitted into the Plan II Honors program at the University of Texas. However, it was not until my 50's, while reading the Bible for the first time, that a true interest in learning emerged. Prior to then, academic excellence was driven by competing with classmates for good grades, and wanting to please authority figures.

Football

Going to High School in Waco, Texas in 1955 was an advantage for athletes hoping for a college scholarship. We were the only white high school in a city of 80,000 residents. Waco High was a 5A Division school, so college coaches regularly scouted our games. Most of the first string players on our 1955 football team received college scholarships.

In 1955 the NCAA ruled that football players must play both offense and defense. The rationale was that larger schools such as the University of Texas had too great of an advantage. The larger, better funded schools were able to provide enough scholarships to play two-platoon football while the smaller schools like Rice University, by default, had to play many of their players the entire game.

The NCAA experiment was not successful as it hurt the quality of the game. Players would tire, fewer players got to play college football and games were less exciting. However, for me, having been selected an all-state end on both offense and defense, the rule resulted in my being heavily recruited. I was already in medical school when four years later the rule was reversed.

The excitement of a senior year in high school combined with the recruitment process made the year pass rapidly. Growing up in Waco, I had not been exposed to the things I saw when visiting the colleges. Going to Dallas' Lou Ann's and Austin's Dessau Hall were delightful eye openers. My first visit to the University of Texas didn't go well. Texas was in the final stage of completing a new dorm for their athletes. Until it was finished, athletes were living in temporary quarters. It was a shock to spend the night there. Many of the sheetrock walls had been removed because the players were regularly breaking them with their fists and heads. The football team had a reputation for fist fighting. It sounded like the wild west. One of the linebackers was known for accepting challenges from local or statewide toughs in bare knuckle fistfights. People would gather to watch a planned fight at a local restaurant parking lot.

Thinking I might avoid the fight scene, I called a girl who lived in Austin whom I had met at a student government conference. We went out on a date and as I had driven to Austin in my new car, we ended up at a local drive-in theatre. About half way through the show, the doors of my car flew open and her boyfriend and four of his friends jumped me. After a few shoves, I proposed we could settle our differences after I took her home. Buying time might present a way to get word to the Texas athletic dorm where the guys would be eager to join the fray. Unfortunately, the boyfriend would not go along with this. He was going to take her home himself. I asked her what she wanted to do, and held my breath. She decided to go home with him. One year later as a freshman at the University of Texas I called her again. We went out after she assured me she wasn't going steady. We didn't return to the drive-in.

Visiting Rice University was quite a contrast. Instead of arranging for other football players to take me out, the coaches arranged for a non-athlete student, Bob Johnson, to take care of me. Bob was a freshman premed major and he got me a date with the prettiest girl at Rice. Bob and I later became good friends when we both were in the 1958 freshman class at Baylor Medical School. I liked Rice a lot. It really impressed to hear that one of the football players, All American Dickey Maegle, was dating movie star, Kim Novak.

Subsequent visits to UT were more enticing than the first. The temporary dorm was torn down and a state of the art college dorm, Moore-Hill Hall, was reserved for UT athletes. It had its' own cafeteria and cook, a woman named Ma Grief. The football practice field and Memorial Stadium were less than a block away.

The coaches arranged for Garland Kennon, an upper classman tackle and high grade point engineering student to show me around. Garland was the largest player in the Southwest conference at that time, weighing 256 pounds. I was admitted to Plan II, a liberal arts honors program that would grow into one of the more outstanding degrees in the country. Plan II was a lifesaver for me. English literature and creative writing had been a strength. However, I was poor at spelling and punctuation. Fortunately, Plan II graded on content.

Reflections on Childhood

A reader might wonder why my parents are called by their first names? If you knew my mother, you would easily see how calling her "Jeri" would be comfortable. Even during childhood, we related to her as a peer and friend. The situation with Rosy was a different matter. My sisters and I called him "Daddy" as young children. However, when I came home for Christmas after lettering in football as a tight-end at the University of Texas, Rosy told me, "I'll be damned if I want a house-ape walking around calling me 'Daddy'. From now on call me "Rosy!"

Looking back as a Christian at the stories of my childhood it shocks me to remember how void my upbringing was of spiritual emphasis. Rearing children without the knowledge found in the Bible is a handicap for parents. The instruction God gives for how he wants his human children to relate to Him is a good model for human parents to use with their own children. God loves and protects his children. Loving God and expressing it through prayer, obedience, and good works was not a characteristic of our family. Affection was not as open or direct as is seen today in most Christian families. I don't remember my parents hugging or kissing me or telling me that they loved me. As a result I relate similarly to my own children. This deprives us both from the satisfaction of expressed loving affection.

However, as a child I felt secure and accepting that my parents loved me and were directing and teaching me in my best interest. They kept my role as child in proper perspective. They understood that childhood is not an end unto itself. Their management reflected the healthy goal of growing up children who would be healthy successful adults. A common fault of today's parents is that many judge their self worth by how others rate their children. Another common mistake is substituting making children happy, for building character.

Growing up for my generation was different than todays culture. My father was a strict disciplinarian and my mother was more like a playmate. Parents did not seem to need to be as vigilance to protect their children. People were not as transient. Neighborhoods were less dangerous. It was rare for a stranger to pass through and when they did they were easily identified. In retrospect, it seems our parents overestimated our ability to judge and protect ourselves. Just taking into consideration physical risks I could have had brain injury from being hit in the head with a hatchet, died from a gunshot wound because I was given a shotgun before I had the maturity to use it, had intellectual disability from repeated concussions sustained in sports or been killed while playing "chicken" in my car.

Of even greater consequence is that I grew up without the basic foundation for a relationship with a Heavenly Father that would have sustained me for eternity.

Bible instruction can be a great help for parents and their children. A unique feature of it's 3000 years of wisdom is that it valid even as cultures change. The technology revolution today is so dramatically changing our culture that the Enlightenment from the Dark Ages seems like a drop in the bucket. The Bible's instructions are not complicated. When we have a clear idea of what is right and what is wrong, parenting is greatly simplified. Homes can remain loving havens where children will grow and strengthen, buffered from the immorality, crudeness, and cruelty displayed by the media. The more fixed children can become in their home-ingrained value system, the better they can withstand an immoral world.

There is no book of childrearing instruction for building character that is so specific, so concise, so well tested, or so available, as the Bible. My book, Biblical Parenting, A Child Psychiatrist's View, ISBN 9781450526951, sorts out the Bible's most relevant instruction. However, this is no substitute for reading the whole Bible.

Below are some of my conclusions for successful child rearing. These ideas are taken from previous writings done after "I got religion." How my childhood measured up to my own published retrospective analysis are put in parenthesis:

Rules For Successful Child Rearing:

•Worship God. A strong spiritual life will lead to a loving and effective family life. (My childhood was weak in this area.)

•Marry for life. Parenting is meant to be a two-person job. (Our parents were never separated or divorced.)

•The most effective way to influence your children is to spend time with them and be a good example. (Not a strong positive influence. My father was a heavy drinker and my mother, though loving and fun, was not a very strong individual.)

•Honor your father and mother. This is the basis for children developing respect for authority. (The greatest strength of my childhood, having proper respect for authority, I feel was the key for my achieving worldly success. It lessens your resistance from learning from elders and makes you more appreciated by those in power. The Bible says if you honor your mother and father you will have a long and good life, Exodus 20:12)

•Discipline is part of love. Do not permit your children to be defiant. (A strong component of our growing up experience.)

•Establish a routine for your children's bedtime, eating habits, and personal hygiene before they are six years old. (A very useful thing for both parents and children. Our childhood was only "fair" in this area)

•Teach your children they are important because God loves them; confidence and self-esteem will follow. (Non existent. Our self esteem seemed to come primarily from our parents' love and winning approval from worldly adults and peers)

•A parent's love, like God's, should be forgiving but there should be consequences for bad behavior. (Our parents were fair and gave consequences, but God's role was not acknowledged)

•More "quality time" with children should not cause the "quantity" of time to decrease. (Not given consideration)

•Limit sleep-overs to special occasions. (Sleep-overs were not popular at Waco in our time)

23

•Seek opportunities for you and your children to pray together. (Never)

•Raise your children in an environment where they will have other positive role models. Participate in church activities. (Seldom)

•Make meals together a family routine and carefully protect this time. (Usually we had Sunday meal together but other times were hit and miss. This was usually because the parents had activities that interfered, not the children.)

•Teaching your children to "make the right choices" is no substitute for parental judgment and protection. Children can understand danger before they have the maturity and self-control to avoid it. (Our parents allowed more independence than we had the maturity to handle.)

•Know your children, their friends, and activities, well enough to judge when to protect, and when to let go. (They knew our friends and their families)

•Make home a secure "base" for your children, but also prepare them to safely move out into the adult world. (parents were pretty good in this area)

•Wealth creates special challenges in being an effective parent. Wealthy parents must not delegate the work of parenting. (We lived like we were wealthy but this did not particularly influence parenting)

•Require, as one condition for sending children to college, that they regularly attend church. (You got to be kidding?)

•If your goal is to raise children the way God would like, study God's parenting manual, the Holy Bible. (Nope)

Bottom line: I look back on my childhood with pleasure and a sense of humor placing no blame on my parents for my own deficiencies and less than satisfactory behaviors and character. I picture my father as a strong, aggressive, competitive, masculine, role model, He was a man's man and I am grateful that in later life we became good friends. My mother was a cute, charming, fun loving character who always made me feel like I was the best thing that ever happened to her. She lived until 101 and still considered me as the "son that shines."

It has taken 79 years for me to appreciate that my survival, success, and good fortune was not at my own direction and self reliance. Thank God He had the patience to protect and guide me.

College Age

You may have noticed that in discussing my own growing up I wrote about childhood, then about college age, without mentioning the adolescent period. This was done to emphasize my view that children are slower to mature these days. Because an adolescent may be so sophisticated using technology, parents can overestimate or misjudge their teenager's maturity level. My clinical experience and psychological testing also show that todays adolescents function more child-like than adult-like.

For being in college in the 50's, my degree of independence seemed about right for my maturity level. Most parents who knew me would have agreed that I had the maturity to make right decisions. Little did they, or I, know how close I would veer toward danger during the times when I had no supervision.

On September 1, 1955, I reported to the University of Texas athletic department and began 2/day practice. In those days the NCAA did not allow freshman to play varsity football. Freshmen had a separate league. Being in the Southwest Conference we were the Texas Shorthorns, playing the Baylor Cubs, the Rice Owlets, etc. We played on Thursday nights. We also sometimes scrimmaged the varsity or ran their opponents' plays.

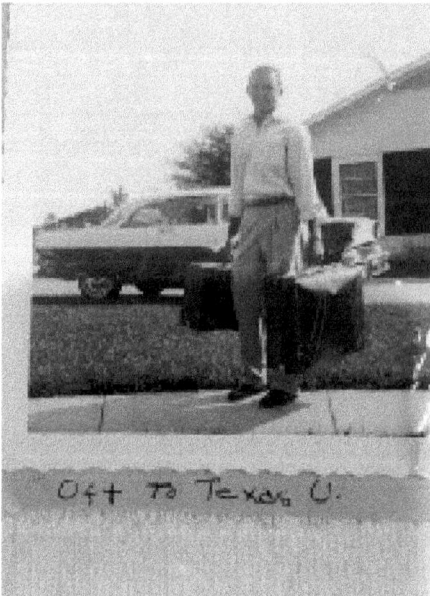

Off To Texas U.

August 1995 - Heading to Austin for the start of football at the University Texas in my new Ford Victoria, a gift from my parents.

Football players all lived in the same dorm and had player roommates. Colleges and Universities were segregated and no black athletes were allowed in the dorms or on the team. No black students were permitted entrance at any Southwest Conference Schools (Texas, Arkansas, Southern Methodist, Baylor, Rice, A&M, and TCU. Texas Tech was admitted in May 1956.)

Ed Price was the Texas head coach from 1951 through the 1956 season. During his tenure his win percentage was 54.9 and in the years that I played, 1955 and 1956, his job was in jeopardy. I later heard that there was dissension between the assistant coaches, some who were vying for his job. None of this at the time was a focus for me as my energy was directed at defending my starting position and keeping my grades up for medical school. In 1957 when Darrell Royal became head coach I could not start the season as I was ill with infectious hepatitis. The short time I worked out with the team after being medically approved for full contact, I could see there was a distinct difference and improvement in the intensity of all aspects of the program.

Football is much different today than in the 1950's. Imagine what today's games would be like if all the African American players were removed? Another difference was that no football teams had weight conditioning. Using weights was limited to re-conditioning of injuries. It wasn't against the rules, it was that no one had thought of it yet. Another difference was that trainers and coaches seldom measured or considered an individual's statistics. Running speed, bench press, vertical jump, the distance one could throw a football, and highlight playing films were not used to ana-lyze a players potential for playing at a higher level. There were no tryout combines. Coaches scouted teams' playing during the high school season and asked other coaches about players of interest.

College teams had little or no off-season training. At Texas we were encouraged to play handball and given a summer running program. During no time after the regular season were we worked out or grilled by coaches. We had spring training which lasted a month, and reported September 1 for two-a-day workouts, usually two weeks before school began. This schedule, or lack thereof, was typical for all Division One schools. Lower Division and high schools were even less regimented.

Soon, technology facilitated measuring and record keeping and the game became more scientific. Coaches like Darrell Royal were quick to use these new tools and such men were instrumental in revolutionizing the game.

Freshman football was even more low pressure. There was a lot of kidding and horseplay. My parents had a house on Lake Belton, about 60 miles from Austin. We had a houseboat painted orange and white named Bevo. It was a frequent destination for us to spend spare time. One weekend, my friend Vince Matthews, our quarterback, and I were at the lake house, when seeing some buzzards in the area, we decided to try to shoot one. My little sister, Fritzi, happened to be there that weekend and we convinced her to lay on a flat rock ledge and pretend to be dead.

Sure enough a big buzzard flew down to take a closer look and we brought him down with a 12 gauge shotgun. He was only wounded so we put him in a big cardboard box and took him back to Austin.

I am ashamed to admit the torment we caused that poor bird as we used it to scare the pants off of other players and coeds. We ended up spray-painting him gold, said he was an eagle, and took him to a fraternity toga party. He was a big hit until some of the more mature members chastised us and took him away and put Mr. Buzzard out of his misery.

My sophomore year, the coaches decided not to redshirt me as Texas was thin at end. Early in the season both of the first string ends went down with knee injuries. By the time of our first conference game with Baylor, I was starting at left end. It was a great thrill to play in the Baylor stadium where so many of my Waco friends and family would attend.

The 1956 University of Texas football team record was not good. Our final record was nine losses and one win. I guess our greatest contribution to University of Texas football was that our record precipitated a coaching change and Darrell Royal came to Texas.

Our opening game in 1956 was with the University of Southern California. It was the first time a Texas team had played an opponent who had an African American player. He was a running back named C.R. Roberts. I remember attending a meeting called by the team captains to discuss how we were going to teach him a lesson for "intruding into our territory." The following is how Wikipedia reports the result of that confrontation: "At the University of Southern California, Roberts led the Trojans to a 44–20 victory over Texas during the 1956 season. It was the first time a black player competed against a white player in that state. He rushed for 251 yards in only 12 minutes and was cheered as he left the field."

I was the first end or back at the University of Texas to wear a face mask. No, we didn't wear leather helmets. Our helmets were plastic and looked similar to the ones that are still being worn. However, in 1956 backs and ends would not put a face mask on their helmet as we thought it would interfere with our ability to catch the ball. This is particularly ironic as in those days passing was not an important part of the game.

One day in practice I was on the bottom of a pileup looking face to face at another player when a foot struck him in the mouth. The cleats peeled his teeth from his gums and onto the ground as if they were kernels of corn.

That day after practice I went to our trainer, Frank Medina, and asked him to put a clear plastic bar on my helmet that would protect my face.

The following week a head to head collision with an SMU player knocked us both unconscious. My face mask was shattered and the netting inside the helmet was torn loose. I am convinced that if I had not been wearing a face mask I would have suffered multiple facial fractures. The coach sent me back in the game but I remember nothing after the collision.

Sophomore 1956
publicity picture

Mexico (Summer of 1956)

Dr. Wilson Crosthwait, the Waco High School football team doctor, was a friend of the owner of Hacienda Santa Engracia, a large ranch near Ciudad Victoria in Tamaulipas, Mexico. The hacienda reportedly was given to the Martinez family by the King of Spain. Originally it was thousands of acres and included a portion of the Sierra Madre Mountain range. During the Agrarian Revolution Poncho Villa fought successfully against the family and a large portion of the hacienda acreage was given to the peasants who had been working in servitude for the owners. Over time, these peasants were unable to sustain their property and functionally they returned to the feudal system that had existed prior to Poncho Villa's war. By the 1950's, the owner, Jose Martinez Gomez ruled as king of the hacienda and his people.

Dr. Crosthwait regularly visited the Hacienda to hunt and fish. During one of these visits evidently Don Jose and Dr. Crosthwait were drinking tequila and waxing poetic, when Jose mentioned he wished he could instill in his two boys, ages six and eight, American values such as tenacity, toughness, determination, competitiveness and aggression. Dr. Crosthwait said he knew just the guy.

Shortly thereafter a letter from Don Jose was delivered to the athletic dorm, Moore Hill Hall, asking me to come to Mexico the next summer to develop a camp for his two sons and their two friends from Monterrey. My answer was a quick affirmative. Experience with Don Jose later showed he was accustomed to moving quickly. When a man functions as a king, he has an idea and it is done. There is no need to take it to a committee for approval. He answered to no committee, but it could be guaranteed his plan had been approved by his strong willed wife, Donna Alicia.

After finishing Football Spring Training in 1956 work I began developing the camp program. Lists of equipment needed for the planned activities of rifle shooting, archery, hunting, fishing, fencing, crafts, baseball, football, track, horseback riding, swimming, and water skiing were made. Ribbon awards for first through fourth place and also trophies were ordered. Don Jose was liberal with the camp budget and he also gave me a list of special things he wanted. Most of his personal requests had to do with transporting guns and ammunition into Mexico.

He ran a hunting concession for tourists at the Hacienda and usually had guns and rifles being repaired in the states. Ammunition was much cheaper in the US than Mexico so he he had me pick up guns and cases of shells. He told me to put these materials under the back seat of my car and if they were discovered at the border to give the inspectors $10.00 or more if necessary and he would reimburse me. What a contrast to way things are now. Today someone crossing into Mexico with hidden guns and ammunition would end up in prison for years. For Don Jose in 1956 it was business as usual.

My salary was never discussed but after each summer camp ended he would give me $600. This was more money than would have been saved doing construction in Waco. While in Mexico there were no living expenses and enjoying such a unique Mexican resort would have been worth it, even without pay.

In the first week of June 1956 my 1955 Ford Victoria, given to me by my parents as a graduation present, was loaded with camp materials and headed to Mexico. Thinking back, it is amazing that my parents were so comfortable with me going to the Hacienda. There were no cell phones in those days and we didn't even know how a telephone call could be made from one country to another. The only phone at the hacienda was in the business office, a separate building.

Two semesters of Spanish at Texas was my total linguistic preparation, my employer and I and had never met, and there were no pictures of the Hacienda for me to view. The one security we had was the confidence that Dr Wilson Crosthwait would not put me in a situation that was bad for me. I drove from Waco, Texas to Monterrey Mexico, 479 miles the first day.

As predicted, at the Laredo border crossing, the guns and ammunition were discovered. The Mexican agent, after given $10 accepted the explanation that they were being transported to Jose Martinez for hunting purposes. The Rio Grande bridge was crossed and soon I was on my way to Monterrey via the Pan American highway. What was not expected was that the police had set up a roadblock between Laredo and Monterrey. They seemed to be waiting for me, went directly to the back seat, and found the guns. The same explanation and $20 and I was back on the road.

The first night in Mexico was spent in a nice hotel in down town Monterrey, where 20 years previously my parents had stayed on their honeymoon. Leaving Monterrey early the next morning was a struggle as the Pan American highway wasn't easily identified. Its route through Monterrey City was not well marked and even when located it was often difficult to ascertain where it proceeded. It was called the Pan American Highway because the proposed route ran through Mexico, Central America, then South America. Reportedly, the further one traveled south the worst the road was maintained. The Mexico segment I travelled was just two lane asphalt. Gas stations were far between and no highway patrol was ever seen.

My instructions were to continue south from Monterrey for approximately 300 miles until reaching a bridge crossing the Purification River. There I would turn right on a gravel road and head toward the Sierra Madre mountains in the distance until arriving at Hacienda Santa Engracia

It took a couple of passes to find the Purification River road. It was one lane, gravel, and serpentine with multiple places where the road had been partially washed away. No other motor vehicles were seen and the only traffic was a rare ox cart or person walking on foot. Only the reassurance from some one walking along the road who pointed further up the road when I asked, "Hacienda Santa Engracia?" kept me from turning back. 20 miles and two and one half hours later, I arrived at the Hacienda.

Hacienda Santa Engracia was a small village with it's main street about 100 yards wide being pinkish sand and gravel. Everything surrounding it was dry, dusty, and desert-like. The main house, the only two story building in the village was of adobe, originally the color of the street but now whitewashed. There were wide concrete steps leading up from the street to a 100 foot long stone porch and the entrance to the main house. The ascending steps were flanked by large date palms. Across the street a small adobe building that served as the hacienda office had a black electrical wire running from the roof of the small office, across the street, to the second floor roof of the main house.

This line ran from a generator in the office and was the only electric line seen in the small village. Across the street from the main house also were several guest houses, one that later served as the boys and my cabin. Behind the cabins ran the pristine Purification River.

I drove my dusty '55 black and white Ford Victoria to the front steps and got out and thought to myself, "I sure as heck am not in Waco."

Main house, Hacienda Santa Engracia, Tamaulipas, Mexico

Down the steps came Don Jose to greet me with a big smile and abrazo (hug). Don Jose was about 50 years old, wearing a big sombrero, Mexican cowboy khakis and boots. He had a ruddy complexion and sported a neatly trimmed blonde mustache.

His pretty dark haired wife, Dona Alicia, in her mid thirties, accompanied him. Behind them came multiple house staff to bring in my bags and equipment. Two American college girls who were spending their summer at the hacienda working as Don Jose's secretaries were also there. Flanking the group, pacing front and rear were two very large gray muscular short haired dogs that appeared to be a Weimaraner/Great Dane mix. The dogs continually roamed the main house grounds keeping unknown people and and farm animals away. They took a quick sniff of me and afterwards related to me as if I belonged there.

Don. Jose Martinez and his two sons,Carlos and Pepe sitting on the steps of Hacienda Santa Engracia. Tamaulipas, Mexico

When the car was unloaded, directions were given to car-ports that were in a barn in back of the main house. My car wasn't seen or driven again until after camp ended in August.

Like many homes in Mexico, the interior of the house was in stark contrast to the drab, hot looking adobe exterior. The inside was elegant with high vaulted ceilings, tile floors, interior gardens, massive dark ebony furniture, and large cavernous rooms.

The walls were adorned with hand painted murals and orig-inal oil paintings. The doors were massive and hand carved. Be-cause of the extraordinarily thick walls, the interior of the house was cool despite the 100 degree outside temperature. All had dec-orative but functional coal oil lanterns on the walls, as there was no electricity in the main house. The one electric line I had noticed crossing the street ran to a separate glass walled contemporary bathhouse and game room. It was air-conditioned but the room was only used on special occasions.

The floor of the main house was used for guests and entertaining. The second floor was the quarters for the family. My quarters, until the camp started, was a large suite located on the first floor in a wing of the main house. The large dining room contained a 40 ft long ebony table. Don Jose sometimes put out cigarettes or built a small fire on this exquisite piece of furniture to demonstrate the extreme toughness of the ebony wood. There was a step-down into a grand library with a huge stone fireplace and walls lined with portraits and armor that were supposedly of Don Jose's medieval relatives. Yep. Definitely I wasn't in Waco.

Don Jose told me that his boys were in Monterrey and wouldn't return for about a month so there would be plenty of time to acclimate and set up the camp program. It was fine with me if he wanted to delay the start. It beat working construction in Mc-Gregor, Texas. Football shoes had been packed and the Hacienda's flat gravel and sand roads with no automobile traffic should be perfect for getting in shape for the fall football season

The two college girls and I ate our meals with the family although I soon began to eat breakfast in the kitchen, as I was usually up earlier than the rest of the family. The food was excellent. The Hacienda produced beef, oranges, and avocados as cash crops. Vegetables, spices, chickens, and beef were homegrown. It was not Tex Mex although every meal was served with home made tortillas, fresh avocados, and refried beans. Breakfast always included fresh squeezed orange juice. The head cook was Lupe, a 60+ year old small thin woman who had been cooking for the family since her childhood.

The first morning I woke up early, put on my running clothes and football shoes and headed down the main street. I remember almost every day wishing that my friends and family could view what I was experiencing. Being on the hacienda was like being in a western movie set in the 1800's. Only oxcart, horse and foot traffic were seen. Coming back into the village from my run there was a big commotion going on.

People were coming out of their houses and frantically running down the street toward the main house. Many were waving their arms motioning for me to follow and shouting, "Ven!" ("Come on!") I joined the crowd, rounded the corner of some buildings near the main house and came to a stable where in an enclosure Don Jose's magnificent black stallion was preparing to mount a frightened looking mare.

The crowd lined the fence joking and shouting words of encouragement. When he was finished, in a very short time, the crowd cheered, clapped, and dispersed. Some of the men slapped me on the shoulder, congratulating me on having the good fortune to be present for this timely event. The thought occurred to me, if this is their big entertainment, what is the rest of my summer going to be like?

After dinner the routine was for us to move to the front porch looking at the stars and talking. Somehow Don Jose could distinguish who the person was by the appearance of his burning cigarette moving along the unlit street. He would whistle and the person would come to him and Don Jose would give the man his orders for the next day's work.

My second evening at the Hacienda Don Jose whistled a man over whom he introduced as Pila, a guide who he said would be taking me up into the mountains the next morning. Although I couldn't understand all the conversation, my impression was that Don Jose had only thought up this project when he recognized Pila walking by. There were a lot of "Si Senors" and Pila disappeared affirming he understood and would carry out Don Jose's instructions. Don Jose said I better go ahead and turn in as Pila would come for me at 6:00 AM the next morning. He said that there was a cabin in the mountains that my campers and I could use on a campout but it had no flooring. He wanted me to floor the cabin. Fortunately for me, but unknown to Jose, I had helped lay down hardwood floors in several houses built by my dad's construction company. I could lay down a floor. I was less sure about going into the wilds of the Sierra Madre mountains with Pila.

Pila knocked on my door at 6:00 AM. He was short, wiry, dark skinned, 60 -70 year old Mexican dressed in cowboy jeans and shirt with a western straw hat. He looked weather beaten and hardened from years of outdoor work. Pila was polite but a man of few words. He directed me to a pickup truck with a driver waiting at the front steps. We got in the cab and traveled an hour along narrow dirt roads toward the Sierra Madre mountains. The landscape changed from desert to tropical by the time we arrived at the mountain foothills. Waiting for us there were several other men with three mules, and two donkeys. Pila and the men unloaded the truck and packed our supplies distributing them over the mules and donkeys.

Two of the mules had Mexican saddles, the type with the large wooden saddle horns. We mounted the saddled mules and Pila headed up the mountain leading the loaded mule and two donkeys. I followed on the other mule.

The Sierra Madre Mountains are an extension of the American Rockies' so the vistas and terrains are very similar. The difference being this area was untamed wilderness. During the six-hour climb and ride we passed one small shack where someone was living. Not being an experienced horseman worried me as some of the paths had dangerous drop-offs. I had never ridden a mule. The two we were riding were larger than most horses, seemed stronger and more surefooted. Supposedly mules had a smoother ride but the climbing motion was for me uncomfortable and painful on the rear.

We arrived at the cabin about 5:00 PM. It was very near the top of the mountain. The cabin was made of logs, had a roof, an opening for windows and a door, but nothing that could be closed. The interior was one room with cross beams on which flooring could be nailed. There was large pile of flooring planks that appeared hand-honed.

Pila unloaded the supplies … hammer, saw, nails, tape measure, level, and L square. There would be barely be time before dark to lay enough flooring for Pila and me to have a place to sleep inside the cabin. As I worked on the floor Pila made a fire, boiled water from a nearby spring, and set out the food he had brought from the Hacienda. He put some grass that grew near the cabin in the boiling water, added some sugar and poured me a cup. It was great! It tasted like hot lemonade.

Having finished preparing the meal, to my surprise, Pila got on his mule and told me he was staying in the little shack we saw halfway down the mountain and that he would come back and check on me every couple of days. He gave me a shotgun and some shells; then he was gone.

Next to worrying about bears, mountain lions, and renegade Mexican Indians, my biggest concern was food. The hacienda had packed multiple buns filled with scrambled eggs and sausage. These were wrapped in a course brown paper about the consistency of toilet paper. Most of the sandwiches were soaked by mule sweat so eating them was out of the question. Avocados, tortillas, oranges, and doves I shot - washed down with lemon grass tea were the food that fueled me the rest of the time in the mountains.

The first night a loaded 12-gauge shotgun and flashlight at my side comforted me enough to sleep through the night on the small patch of finished flooring. Early the next morning, flooring the cabin begun with new intensity. When Pila returned two days later, the cabin was about one half covered.

I did my best to explain to him that when he next returned, to come in the morning. Finished or not, we were going to go back to the Hacienda. Two days later Pila arrived at the cabin at daybreak. The floor was not complete but it was adequate for my four campers and me to use when we returned. We loaded the mules and donkeys, and made it back to the hacienda by nightfall.

Don Jose expressed surprise that I had returned so soon. He said he thought we would have stayed a few extra days to have Pila take me hunting in the Mountains. It had never entered my mind! Shortly before the campers and I took our planned trip to the mountains, the cabin was struck by lightening and burned to the ground.

After returning to the hacienda, my time was spent scouting the facilities and discussing the proposed camp schedule with Don Jose. I met other children in the village who could join us for team sports, and spent my free time running and lifting weights to prepare for fall football. Weight lifting had an interesting twist. In the barn there were what appeared to be 100-pound barbells. It turned out that these were the wheels from a train engine that had been used on a narrow gauge railroad that Don Jose's father had built for Hacienda use. They were perfect for bench pressing.

I also spent time getting to know the two college girl secretaries. The girl's parents came to the hacienda for hunting and fishing trips. On a recent visit the parents mentioned to Don Jose that their daughters had just graduated from college and had no specific plans for the future. He suggested the girls work for him for a month or two while they thought about what they would do. They had been there several weeks and were bored. They told me they wanted to go home early because of Don Jose's cousin, Pedro.

Mexican Gunslinger

Pedro was Don Jose's 60 year old cousin. Although he was an accomplished Mexican artist, he had difficulty with his personal and financial life. Periodically he would come to spend a month or two at the Hacienda, broke and unhealthy from his lifestyle. In exchange for Don Jose's hospitality Pedro painted murals and designed and made furniture for the hacienda. The girls told me Pedro had a crush on them and had become a nuisance by always trying to be with them. They asked me to hang around them some to help keep Pedro at bay. I was happy to oblige.

That night as we went out after dinner to sit on the front porch, just before Pedro sat down next to the girls I took the place where he intended to sit. He was incensed and began swearing. He obviously had been drinking and he started toward me. When he got too close, my hands went up instinctually to stop him. He lost his balance and fell. He got up by himself and stalked away angrily. We continued with our conversations on the porch, not giving the incident much further concern.

This incident happened to occur on the one Saturday a month when there was a dance in the Hacienda village. A generator provided electricity for music and lighting. Sitting on the porch you could hear the loud Mexican ranch music playing down the street. It wasn't the greatest of diversions, but it surely would beat watching horses mate. Elizabeth, one of the college girls, and I decided to walk down the street and check it out.

There were villagers dancing and drinking beer and having a good time. We had a beer and joined the dancers. We had just started to dance when someone slapped me hard on the shoulder. Turning, expecting to have to deal with one of the young guys at the dance, it was a surprise to confront Pedro. He was drunk and said he wanted to "talk to me out in the street." We stepped out into the dusty street, much like in the western movies, and he began to rant and rave about how the Mexicans were a proud people and how he had been insulted in front of his friends and family. The more he talked, the more hysterical he became. He suddenly pulled out a pistol and said he was going to shoot me.

That got my attention! Then a phenomenon occurred that happened again about 50 years later when arrested while on a mission trip to Cuba; my ability to speak Spanish miraculously improved! I apologized, explaining that the push was instinctive, and meant no offense.

Could he possibly hold off on the shooting until we talked it over further tomorrow morning? He said that sounded OK to him and he turned and walked off toward the main house. I went in and got Elizabeth, walked her back to her room and headed toward mine.

Along the way Pedro stepped out from the shadows, waving the pistol saying, he had reconsidered and he was going to shoot me after all. Fortunately, Don Jose heard the commotion, came down stairs, took the gun away from him and sent him to bed. This incident was never mentioned again by Don Jose, Pedro, or myself. Pedro must of gotten over his anger as he later asked me to sit for a portrait.

Nevertheless, it was a relief when Pedro completed his R&R and left the Hacienda to resume his art career. To my disappointment, the girls left about the same time.

Several days after Pedro threatened to shoot me he asked for me to sit for this portrait.

Boredom?

Life on the hacienda was seldom boring. While waiting for the boys to return from Monterrey and for the camp to begin I would often go hunting or fishing. There was a large lake and a river, both of which had excellent bass fishing. Below the dam were groves of trees and a predicable flight path for blue rock pigeons (a wild Mexican bird that looks like a dove but is the size of a pigeon.) All game would be deliciously prepared by Lupe and enjoyed by the family and guests.

Since beef cattle was one of the Hacienda's cash crops, fresh steaks were a common entree. It was less frequent that pork was served. An occasion that precipitated a menu shift happened one afternoon. The two huge dogs I mentioned previously were clearly the front line security in protecting the main house and grounds. They reeked with the pride they felt from having such a responsibility. To their extreme chagrin this particular afternoon a huge hog slipped through the gate into the manicured back yard and bougainvillea lined patio where dinner often was served. Shock and indignant is an gross understatement.

All Hell broke loose! They rushed howling at the hog who in terror ran squealing for his life. He ran straight through the glass wall of the stand alone game room, the only air conditioned room in the house. It was a bloody mess. The dogs were hanging on to him as he thrashed about the room breaking furniture and spewing blood everywhere. I never knew whether the dogs killed him, or he died from cuts going through the glass wall or by a bullet. All I know for sure is that we had pork chops that night. For several days after the dogs were in a very bad mood and we gave them an even wider berth.

Several days after the hog incident there was a big commotion along the street in front of the house. The dusty main street was dotted with people running and shouting similar to the way it was when the mare was being bred. However, this time they were running the opposite direction as if fleeing for their lives.

Instead of shouting, "Come on," they were yelling, "Run Away, Manuel is coming!" In the distance there was a cloud of dust approaching the Hacienda. When it was closer, a jeep with a driver and a man sitting in the back with a pistol in each hand firing into the air could be defined. The jeep roared up to the front porch screeching to a halt and a tall dust-covered Mexican man in tight fitting charro pants with a sombrero and handlebar mustache jumped out of the jeep and rushed up to shake my hand. The hand had a big Texas A&M ring on it!

It was Don Jose's cousin, Manuel, who owned a hacienda nearby. He said he wanted to meet the "T- Sip" that was working at the Hacienda. Manuel and Don Jose had attended Texas A&M together and they had a lot of stories to tell. The kitchen staff later told me a story they didn't mention:

One evening several years previous Manuel was visiting and dinner was being served on the outside patio. Manuel was more intoxicated than usual. In attendance at dinner that night was a young Mexican medical intern who was doing the required government medical rotation of public service at the Hacienda.. In the course of the evening, he questioned Manuel's pistol marksmanship. As the argument became more heated, Manuel made the doctor stand in front of an outside wall of the house holding a glass in his hand. He fired six shots, never hitting the glass or the doctor.

My first summer working at the Hacienda Don Jose bought a plane. He did not know how to fly but intended to take lessons. A landing strip had been prepared about one half mile from the main house. The day it was to be delivered we were all sitting on the front porch waiting. The pilot was to buzz the house as the signal for us to come pick him up and see the plane.

Seeing that the main street was deserted and that we were sitting on the front porch, the pilot decided it would be more impressive to do a fly by. He circled the house, put the plane into a dive, and leveled off several feet above the dirt street and roared past us at eye level. He went under the one wire in the town. The one that ran from the one story office crossing the street going to the roof of the second story of the main house. Pretty impressive!

When we picked up the pilot and Don Jose expressed his admiration, we learned the pilot had never seen the wire. During the three summers I worked at the hacienda, Don Jose never flew his plane.

Another enjoyable diversion for the Hacienda family was attending country fairs. There were food booths, games, music, and Mexican rodeo events. However, the main attraction was horse racing. These were grudge races, usually with only two horses racing. There was local betting but the majority of the money that changed hands came from the horse owners who bet against each other.

Don Jose had a stable of fine thoroughbred horses which he bought in the United States and trained for racing. One family who lived in the village was made up of generations of horse trainers and jockeys. The night before one particularly big race Don Jose invited me to attend his meeting with the jockey where race strategy would be discussed. The jockey was only eleven years old, and was smoking a big cigar. Another twist in the race scenario was the appearance of the beautiful thoroughbred horse. The horse was intentionally not groomed and made dirty in hopes of getting more favorable betting odds.

Following one fair after the Hacienda's horse successfully won the race (and the bet), Don Jose threw a big party. His wife, Dona Alicia, was spending that night at a second home they owned in nearby Ciudad Victoria. Being uninvited to the party did not

keep me from observing and hearing most of the festivities. There
was a Mariachi band, horseback riding and Mexican rodeo type
performances, and lots of alcohol. Toward the end of the evening
Don Jose and four or five of the guests rode their horses up the
steps of the house and then down into the large library. The horseplay progressed and soon the swords and shields were pulled off
the wall and mock battles began. The next morning there was a
mess but no evidence of bloodshed or corpses. Don Jose wasn't
seen until two days later, and he still looked hung over.

Camp

My four campers returned to the Hacienda the first of July.
They consisted of 8 year old Pepe and his younger brother, 6 year
old Carlos, both children of Don Jose and Dona Alicia. The two
other boys were 8 year old Wicho (Morissio) and his 6 year old
brother Gongi (Gonzalo) from Monterrey.

Their parents were good friends of the family. The personalities and dynamics of the boys' interaction with me and themselves would be a book unto itself. I will only mention a few highlights about Camp Hacienda Santa Engracia.

Carlos, Pepe, Wicho. Gongi

The boys were well-mannered, respectful, eager to learn, were no management problem and were a lot of fun. They spoke very little English but I became fluent in Mexican child-speak. The boys were good friends and often would give each other a big hug and call the other affectionately "mi cunado," brother-in-law. The schedules I remembered from Camp Stewart. The setting was perfect for a boys camp. It included a river and a lake for fishing and skiing, fine horses, mountains nearby for hiking and camping, wonderful food, hunting available, and a large staff from the Hacienda to assist.

Village children were recruited for team sports. Everyone had a good time. The most difficult child management times came during horseback riding activities. Even at their young age the children were expert riders; I was not. A favorite diversion for them was to ride full speed into one of the avocado or orange orchards for a game of chase. It was difficult for me to keep up so I would put my horse in a strategic location and yell instructions as they whizzed by. Fortunately no one ever got hurt.

The hacienda had a large lake and several aluminum boats with 10 horsepower Johnson motors used for fishing. The boats were underpowered for skiing but the boys were light so we gave it a try. A young Mexican man, Juan, who worked as a gardener was recruited to help.

Even though the boys were light, it was a struggle for them to get up on the water behind the underpowered boat. Initially I tried having the Mexican helper stay in the water to assist the boys while I drove the boat. Juan had never seen anyone ski and my shouting instructions to him in broken Spanish didn't work well. Next, I tried having him drive the boat while I tried to keep the skiers afloat, with their ski tips up. This was more dangerous as Juan had difficulty controlling the boat with a skier was being dragged behind.

Then, an idea occurred to me. There was a four-foot deep, sixty-foot long lap pool in back of the Hacienda main house. The ski rope and skis and campers were taken to the lap pool. Six Mexican teenagers were located to help. Three of the campers would sit on the edge of the pool watching while the fourth would get into the pool with me. Arranging the fourth camper in the pool with ski tips up, and the rope in-between his knees, was easy as I could stand at his side, not having to swim. On the count of three the six Mexican teens would run fifty feet pulling the ski rope. The camper would be jerked onto top of the water and soon was skiing along the length of the pool. After all the boys were able to get up in the pool, we went back to the lake where they all quickly learned to ski proficiently.

These boys did some things that campers in America would unlikely experience. Once we went on a campout accompanied by Pila, the Indian guide who had taken me up in the mountains. The kitchen prepared our food for the trip. The first part of the trip was in a truck, and the campers rode with Pila in the cab. I rode in the truck bed but I was not alone. In the bed with me was a small pig. Later that afternoon my suspicion was confirmed that I was riding in the back with our dinner.

Few boy scouts in America have roast pig on a campout. Pila butchered the pig out of sight and sound of the boys and me. However, as he brought the piglet prepared for cooking to the campfire in his other hand he was carrying the pigs lungs, both still attached to its trachea. There in the woods he gave us a lesson on pulmonary anatomy and physiology. He would blow into the attached trachea and make the lungs inflate like a balloon. Of course all of us had to give it a try.

The next day we walked up a shallow stream to a place where the river came out of the ground from multiple springs. Near this beautiful site was a stone cliff, going straight up several hundred feet. Attached to the cliff a rusty metal ladder went up about 60 feet where the 20 ft mouth of a cave could be seen on the cliff face. Pila told me that this was an abandoned mine site called the Cueva de Guano (bat feces) for obvious reasons.

The children wanted to climb the ladder to see the mine and bats. It was too dangerous for them but Pila said he would watch the campers while I took a look. During the climb I became aware of a fear of heights. Nevertheless, by not looking down, I made it up the 60 feet and crawled onto the ledge that became the floor going into the cave.

There wasn't much there but an abandoned mine shaft going further into the cliff. Leaving the cave I realized that the ladder did not come above the floor of the cave. The only way to get my feet onto a ladder rung was to scoot backwards on my stomach, hang the lower half of my body over the cliff, then use my legs to feel for a rung. Fifty years later, I break into a cold sweat just thinking about it.

Visitors to the Hacienda

   After the camp would close in August, friends of mine usually would come to the hacienda to visit. From the Hacienda we would make a trip to Mexico City and Acapulco before returning home and back to college.

   In August 1956, two Texas football teammates, Vince Matthews, Arlis Parkhurst, and a University of Texas tennis player, Bill Hinkle, joined me on a road trip to Acapulco. We rotated drivers and traveled both night and day down the Pan American highway to our most important destination, Acapulco. In Acapulco most nights we slept on the beach, and took showers in the rooms of other young people we met.

   In August 1957 my Waco friend, Bill Miller rode with his parents to Monterrey and from there he took a bus to Ciudad Victoria where I met him and drove him back to the Hacienda for several days. The owners of the Hacienda had two teenage girl relatives visiting the family and they arranged dates for Bill and me. The kitchen packed a picnic lunch for us and took us by truck to the beautiful private Purification River swimming hole near where the boys and I had camped. The water was deep and crystal clear. On the far side of the swimming hole was a natural stone ramp that slanted upward from the water about ten feet and then leveled off to form a shelf, perfect for having a picnic lunch. Bill and I swam across the river, keeping the picnic foods out of the water.

   We spread out a tablecloth and arranged the food a la Martha Stewart. The girls then swam across and joined us. It was an impressive, romantic setting.

   As we unpacked our lunch basket the girls pointed out that the picnic basket include their favorite sandwiches, Hacienda Santa Engracia egg and sausage. These were the same type I didn't eat when I was in the mountains and I still wasn't about to have one. Bill, on the other hand, took a sandwich. He started removing the toilet-paper-like wrapping. He toyed with it some but when the girls were not looking he slipped the sandwich into his bathing suit.

   After awhile Bill said he was going back to the other side for something. We watched as he dove off into the crystal clear water below. When Bill hit the water yellow and black scrambled eggs rushed out of the legs of his bathing suit and what appeared to be toilet paper trailed after him as he swam. The scene should be in the hall of fame on "How Not To Impress a First Date."

While I was working in Mexico, I read a book about the training of kamikaze pilots during World War II. It was unimaginably harsh. One aspect of their training stuck in my mind: To improve their reflexes they were required to catch flies out of the air. I was preparing for a college football season and was interested in improving my hand/eye coordination. What better way do it than catch flies, and what better place to catch flies than in Mexico? I became very proficient. Some Mexicans taught me a useful twist. After catching a fly they would throw it forcefully against a hard flat surface such as a wall or bar counter. This would stun the fly so that it could be picked up and put it in a glass of liquid. They would hold the fly under the liquid with a spoon for three or four minutes until it was obviously drowned. Next they would take the fly out of the liquid and put it in an ash tray. There is nothing more dead looking than a soaked wet unconscious fly. Anyone will take a bet that you will not be able to bring the dead fly back to life. After the bets are on the table, you light a cigarette or cigar and sprinkle warm ashes on the dead fly. Soon a small leg will begin to move, then another, and the fly will right itself, shake off the ash and fly away. You pick up the money and leave the bar.

The last time I was in Mexico was in 1983. My son, Dan Jr. and I drove there for a short visit. It had changed greatly. The road to the Hacienda had been paved and the village and main house had electricity. There were styrofoam cups and plastic bottles littering the Purification riverbank. A short time after that visit the Hacienda was sold. It is now a hotel and resort. Both Don Jose and Dona Alicia are deceased. The older son, Pepe who was marked to be the future Don Jose of the Hacienda died in his forties of cancer of the breast. Carlos has a small orange orchard and lives with his wife in one of the casitas that the campers used. A younger daughter, Alicia, had become the manager of the Hacienda. Wicho and Gongi, I have been told, are successful businessmen in Monterrey.

Reflections on Mexico Experience

Writing about these escapades brings to mind how dangerous these trips must seem to the reader. It also calls the great difference between the culture of the 1950's and today. We were four strong athletic, fun loving young men with no malicious intent. We felt we could defend ourselves if necessary and assumed no one would mess with four of us. In those days Mexico was not rife with drug lords, gangs, kidnappings, or terrorists. Our world had not suffered the loss of moral fiber evident today. Neither the United States or Mexico had regressed to today's decadence.

The attitudes and behaviors of young people in the 1950's were more civilized. Growing up in Texas, there were some times when conflict between two teenage boys became so intense that we would "fight it out." We called it "fighting fair." Only the two boys with the disagreement would fight. For two or three to jump on one was seen as cowardly. No weapons were used. For one boy to attack another with a club or bat would have been unthinkable. There would be no scratching or biting. Most of us had never heard of Karate, and kicking was not allowed. Once your adversary was down, the fight was over. Never, never, would it have occurred to someone to kick their opponent when he was on the ground.

Today's youth would laugh at our rules for a "fair" fight. I read of two teenagers from a prestigious Dallas high school, meeting to fight over a girl. One had a friend with him, the other brought several. Ten to fifteen boys attacked two boys, eventually clubbing, and kicking them to the ground where one of the teenagers then tried to gouge out his rival's eyes.

Law officers will tell you their most dangerous task is arresting an armed teenager. Our children are less civilized. Some of them have become savages.

When my friends and I made our Mexico trip we were immature, goofy, had poor judgement but we were not savages. If our parents had been better informed about what we were doing they would not have permitted us to go.

Actually, being immature, goofy, and having poor judgement is enough to get you in plenty of trouble. Particularly if you are in a foreign country, don't speak the language, and are are drinking alcohol. On one leg of the trip toward Mexico City, I am ashamed to admit, we were driving under the influence of alcohol on a mountain road when we stopped to pick up rocks to throw at highway signs and stray goats from our moving car. We were fortunate we did not have an accident an accident. Our irresponsible vandalism could have had severe percussions. If we had been seen by the Mexican police, we would have been arrested and spent time in a Mexican jail.

Looking back, my attitude and approach to my Mexico adventures were naive and simple minded. This was brought home to me recently from reading the novel, All the Pretty Horses by Cormac McCarthy. The story took place in the 1950's, the same time period that I was working on an hacienda in Mexico. In the novel three Texas teenagers rode horses across the Rio Grande river into similar areas where I was galavanting. There were not as fortunate as I. They ran into unscrupulous, sadistic, Mexican lawmen with the result they ended up in primitive Mexican prisons where one barely survived a prison knife fight and another was executed.

Think about it. I had been stopped twice by Mexican police for smuggling guns and ammunition, should have been arrested for destruction of Mexican road signs, and twice was accosted by an enraged drunken Mexican on a time-forgotten hacienda where all law and order was managed by the gunman's cousin. All this was endured with a simple Devil-may-care attitude, unscathed. Why would God have protected such a irresponsible, irreverent, creature? I must have been assigned a full time guardian angel.

Playing Football for Darrell Royal

Darrell Royal came to the University of Texas in 1957 for spring training. It was a different ball game. Under Ed Price, blue chip players, unless injured, were pretty sure they would be starters. With Coach Royal all positions were up for competition. No one could rest on his laurels. The person who worked the hardest and rated the best in practice each week would be the person who would be playing in the game. Ranking of players were posted daily. I was one of the few lettermen that Coach Royal inherited. It didn't matter, with Coach Royal you earned your spot in the present.

I did have one advantage. In games we had to play both offense and defense, Coach Royal chose his team primarily on defensive toughness. His theory was that if someone was a hitter, he could teach them to play offense. Defense was my forte. I was looking forward to the competition and playing out my two years of remaining varsity eligibility under Coach Royal. However, before the fall of 1957, Darrell Royal's first season as Texas coach, my life took two unexpected turns.

Turn One - Infectious Hepatitis

After Hacienda Santa Engracia Camp finished in August 1957, Bill Miller, my friend from Waco joined me on a trip to Mexico City and Acapulco. Driving back to Texas, I became quite ill with heavy vomiting, fever, and dehydration. By the time we reached Waco I had become a bright shade of yellow. Dr. Crosthwait diagnosed me with infectious hepatitis and admitted me to isolation in Waco Hillcrest Hospital Returning to Texas in mid September, playing football was not a possibility. I was so weak I could barely walk to class. My weight when school ended in May 1957 was 192 pounds. When I returned in September, three months later, my weight was 152. I had lost 40 pounds!

In December 1957 I was medically cleared to return to football. Surprisingly, my weight was back up to 192 pounds. Texas was going to meet the University of Mississippi in the Sugar Bowl. I started running Mississippi team's plays as the last end on the depth chart. By the time the varsity left for New Orleans I had advanced enough to make the trip. However I couldn't go as playing even one down would have forfeited a year's eligibility. With two more years' eligibility, I was excited and confident I would soon be playing regularly for Coach Royal.

Turn Two – Baylor Medical School

In mid March 1958 I went to Houston to visit Dr. Crosthwait's son, Bobby, who was a senior student at Baylor Medical School. Bobby showed me around and introduced me to Dean James Schofield. Dr. Schofield said that it was the last day Baylor was interviewing applicants to Baylor. He suggested that I go through the interviews even though my plans were to play two more years of football. He said it would be good practice. I didn't think the interviews went particularly well and returned to Austin not giving the visit in Houston much significance with spring training being on my mind.

One week later a letter arrived in my UT mailbox from Dean Schofield saying I had been accepted to Baylor Medical School, the class of 1962 and was to report to class Monday September 7, 1958. I had never formally applied! Acceptance was conditional on me satisfactorily completing the required pre med courses during the summer. How this all came about, is still a mystery to me.

This was a time when Baylor Medical School was the only Texas medical school that could admit applicants from out of state. It was aggressively competing highly rated east coast medical schools when striving for student diversity was popular. Maybe not many other schools were admitting football players? Also, I suspected that Dr. Crosthwait might have had something to do with it. I had to decide if I would leave the University of Texas and forfeit my two years of Texas football eligibility. My Dad encouraged me to go on to medical school.

I went to talk to Coach Royal about this turn of events. I expressed how getting into medical school was extremely important to me but that letting him and my teammates down by not playing out my eligibility bothered me greatly. Coach Royal said he understood and appreciated my concern. He said he would like for me to stay, but that at 6 foot, 192 pounds it was unlikely I would have a career in pro football as a defensive end. He wished me well in medical school and said he would keep me on scholarship for the remainder of the semester.

At the time it never occurred to me that the decision to go on to medical school would have an important personal health implication. Being somewhat underweight for an end, I made up the deficit by aggressive play and hard hitting. In those days it was legal and taught by coaches to "spear" your opponent with your head when tackling or blocking. On several occasions I had played games not remembering anything after a hard hit. No one knew then that repeated concussions could lead to permanent brain injury. If I had played out my eligibility my Med Cat scores might have been lowered sufficiently to exclude me from medical school.

God must have wanted me to be a doctor. I certainly didn't thank him at the time. From my spiritually blind perspective, being forced to make such a choice was somewhat unfair. It never occurred to me that God was directing my future, working in my best interest, and that He had plans for me that were beyond my understanding.

For 20 years I regularly had dreams about returning to The University of Texas to play out my eligibility. One night I dreamed Coach Royal said, "Dan, you are almost 40 years old. Come back as an assistant coach if you want. You are too old to play football." That was the last time I ever had that dream.

In 1960 I attended the Texas/ Syracuse national championship game at the Cotton Bowl in Dallas. At half time I went down on the field to talk to some of my Texas Cowboy friends who were in the end zone guarding the University of Texas cannon. When the Texas football team ran onto the field with Coach Royal leading them, he saw me. He peeled off from the team, came up, shook my hand, and asked me how medical school was going. It did more to dissuade the guilt I harbored about leaving early than years of psychotherapy could have done. Several weeks after graduation from Baylor Medical School a letter of congratulations was received from Coach Royal.

Through the years when I have seen Coach Royal at letterman reunions and social events he has always treated me as an important team member and expressed pride in my being a physician. What a fine man he was!

Medical Student and Marriage

In 1958, Baylor College of Medicine was in its heyday. Dr. Michael DeBakey and Dr. Denton Cooley were fierce competitors as world-renowned surgeons. Both were professors at Baylor Medical School. Students in their clinical training years had direct contact with them in the operating room, holding contractors, cutting sutures and being subjected to terrifying impromptu in-surgery quizzes.

The first two years of medical school were spent from 8:00 AM to 5:00 PM in the classroom. On the first day of class, Dean Schofield addressed us by saying, "Look at the student on either side of you. That person you see will be graduating with you four years from now. Your class of 84 students was selected from 1000 applicants from all over the United States. We have invested too much in you to allow you to fail. Four years from now you will be a doctor."

My first year of medical school may have tested Baylor's formula. Three years as an undergraduate at the University of Texas never developed in me a mature study ethic. Having good native intelligence and great stamina got me by at Texas. These are excellent traits for a physician to possess but not enough to make an outstanding medical student.

At the University of Texas, I dated but had no serious romantic relationships. My tendency was to like pretty girls who were unavailable. One of these pretty girls was Yvonne Brown, who was engaged to my roommate, Mike Trant, a senior and Captain of the 1956 football team. At second semester in 1957 Mike moved out of the athletic dorm and into the Phi Delta Theta fraternity house. After graduation, Mike became a Marine pilot.

My first day at Baylor medical school, I ran into Yvonne. She had graduated from the University of Texas at mid term and was working in the Department of Microbiology. Yvonne told me she and Mike had broken up and that night I took her out on a date. One year later we were married.

Highland Park Presbyterian Church
June 5, 1959

Joan McKnight, Francis French, Kay Campbell, Ann Griffin,
Yvonne Brown, Janet Spies, Nancy Myers, Jan Armstrong
Arlis Parkhurst, Bill Hinkle, Bill Miller, Joe Flood, Dan Myers,
Richard Keeton, Tommy Flood, Vince Matthews

My first year of medical school was a challenge. Yvonne and I had spent enough time together to decide we would get married and in addition I had to put in enough hours to satisfactorily get through that grueling first year. Despite the competing demands of courtship, marriage, and medical school, only one "letter" was received while at Baylor. A letter is a notice from a professor that a student's performance on an exam is weak enough that an appointment must be scheduled to discuss the teacher's concerns. Ironically, my letter was in psychiatry, the specialty that eventually became my career.

Final exams the first year came one week before our marriage date. My study time was compromised by prenuptial activities. It was stressful. An upper class man advised me to forget studying psychiatry. He said the Psychiatry Department always asked the same question, "Discuss the Importance of Treating the Patient as a Whole." He was confident I could come up with ideas to answer the question without studying.Baylor final exams were comprehensive (covered everything taught since entering medical school) and essay rather than multiple choice. During the exam I left the psychiatry question to last. I titled my psychiatry essay and wrote several pages expanding on points the upper class man had told me Psychiatry liked to hear.

When the Chairman of the Department of Psychiatry, Dr. Ken Ross Wright, called me into his office, he seemed truly puzzled as he reviewed my exam answer with me. It turned out "Treating the Patient as a Whole" was not the question they had asked, and to his consternation, he pointed out that I had misspelled my essay title, "Treating the Patient as a Hole." Nevertheless, he liked what I said in the essay and he had a sense of humor.

Our honeymoon was three months at the Hacienda Santa Engracia. I ran the boy's camp and Yvonne worked as Don Jose's secretary and receptionist. Two more campers were added and I had an assistant counselor, Tommy Husbands, from Waco. This allowed me to sleep in quarters with Yvonne while Tommy bunked with the campers.

As a result of this arrangement, on March 25th, 1960 the Baylor Medical School chairman of the Department of Obstetrics in Houston delivered our daughter Simone. She was the first birth in our class so she received a lot of attention from classmates. Her picture appeared in our school yearbook. On November 24, 1961 our second daughter Yvette was born.

Medical school graduation was in May 1962. I had been elected president of our senior class and gave a well-received but somewhat maverick speech at graduation. It was a takeoff on my mother-in-law's comment that an MD degree was a "license to steal."

Dan A. Myers, MD   Baylor Medical School
Graduation - May 1962

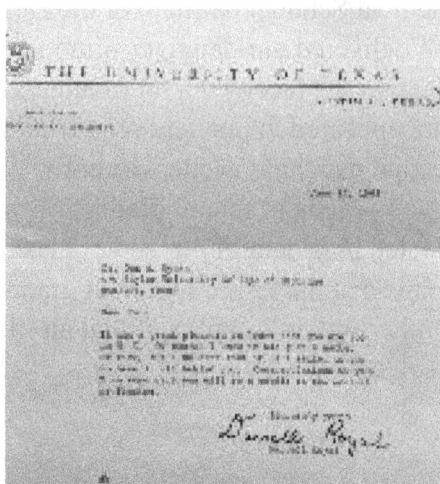

Letter from Coach
Darrell Royal

(More legible rendering of Coach Royal's letter)

June 22, 1962

Dr. Dan A. Myers
℅ Baylor University College of Medicine
Houston, Texas

Dear Dan:

It was a great pleasure to learn that you are now an M. D.
Of course I knew it was just a matter of time, but I am sure it is a
relief to you to have it behind you. Congratulations to you. I am
sure you will be a credit to the medical profession.

Sincerely yours

Darrell Royal

Darrell Royal

Internship

My internship was at Methodist Hospital in Dallas. My first rotation was in Radiology. The first morning of the internship I began by observing radiological procedures and standing by in case there was a need for a general medical physician. The first case was a woman who was to have an exam by fluoroscopy. The radiologists were accommodating for fluoroscopy by wearing red glasses before the procedure began. The patient was waiting on a stretcher and two radiologists with their glasses in place were talking affably.

Stopping to say "hello" to the patient, to my horror, I saw, as I was not wearing red glasses, that she was bright red, covered head to toe by a rash. As I moved to get the radiologist's attention, she began to gasp for breath. The very first hour of my internship had begun with diagnosing and treating a patient who was in anaphylactic shock, an allergic reaction to chemicals given intravenously for improving the images during fluoroscopy. It is potentially a fatal event. Fortunately the patient survived.

Several weeks later while I was on duty at the hospital, there was a frightening emergency at our home. Our daughter, one year old Yvette, was crawling across the floor and touched the metal stand of the TV while her bare foot was in contact with the floor furnace. Electricity surged through her. As a dime size hole was burned through her hand, she convulsed and stopped breathing. Yvonne picked her up and ran with her into the street, stopped a car, and asked the driver to take her to the Parkland Emergency Room. When they arrived at the Emergency Room the doctor told me that when Yvonne had put Yvette on the table, Yvette began to breathe and her heart began to beat.

The doctors said that Yvonne, rocking Yvette back and forth on her chest, had done a form of CPR, saving her life. After the electric shock, Yvette, who had been rather sluggish, compared to Simone seemed more animated. She has gone on to get a Masters degree in Engineering and an MBA.

I remember reading somewhere that people who had survived being hit by lightening develop new attributes and different personality characteristics. I wouldn't recommend it, but it seemed to give Yvette a jumpstart.

In joke-telling, timing is everything. The best-timed joke I have ever heard occurred during my internship while I was on call at the hospital It was in October 22, 1962 during the Cuban Missile crisis. There were five of us interns gathered in the Doctor's lounge glued to the television watching live as Soviet ships loaded with missiles continued to sail directly into the United States naval blockade of Cuba. Soviet and American missile crews were on full alert. We realized that if the Russian ships did not turn back within minutes, the US Navy would open fire on them, and both Russia and America would let go of their intercontinental nuclear weapons. The tension in the doctors lounge was so great you could cut it with a knife. At this crucial moment, one of the more respected senior staff doctors came into the room and gave us the following advice: "Should Dallas be targeted you must make every effort to survive the initial blast. When the sirens sound, find a cushioned chair, move it so the back of the chair faces toward any glass windows. Remember to remove your eyeglasses, and put them under the seat cushion. Do the same with any pens in your shirt pockets. Close your eyes tightly and do not open them until the flash subsides. Hold your breath and put your arms over your ears and bend forward as far as you can with your head tight between your legs. Then, …….he paused for effect, "Kiss your ass good bye!"

My internship, which took place from July 1962 to June 1963 was fast paced. It often would be 36 hours "on" at the hospital and only 12 "off" at home. At Methodist, a private hospital, there was a clear relationship between how hard and long you worked and the number of procedures the attending doctor would allow you to assist or complete. I worked extra, got to deliver a good many babies, assist in multiple surgeries, took out a few appendixes, and received an Outstanding Intern Award.

Yvonne and I had rented a house in the area where she had grown up, the Park Cities in Dallas. Yvonne was an only child and the house we rented was next door to her parents. The extra support they provided likely explains how our children emerged unscathed from a year of a father who usually was absent.

Medical Corps, U.S. Army

In 1963 the United States was at war with Vietnam and there was a doctors draft. The war was not supported by a lot of our countrymen. Young physicians unsuccessfully tried to avoid being called away from their medical training or practice. When I received my draft notice to report to an army office in downtown Dallas for my physical exam, I thought I might have an ace in the hole. It hadn't been that long since I played football at Waco High School. My parents still lived in Waco and had local connections. It seemed advantageous to me to report to Waco where I would be known, than to report to Dallas where I would be just a number.

On the designated physical examination day I left the hospital at 5:00 AM, drove 100 miles to Waco and checked into the Waco recruiting office at 7:00 AM. There were about 25 of us filling out papers until 8:00 AM. At that time we were marched out of the building onto a bus where we were driven 100 miles to the downtown Dallas office for our physical exam and then back to Waco. So much for special connections.

Two short weeks later I received notice from the US Army that on July 1, 1963 I was to report to the Medical Field Service School at Ft. Sam Houston in San Antonio, Texas for orientation and basic training, following which I would join, as a Battalion Surgeon, the First Armored Division preparing for deployment to Vietnam. This was beginning to sound serious!

The month at the Medical Field Service School in San Antonio was like a scene from the television show MASH. My group consisted of about five hundred young doctors, none of them wanting to be in the Army, all trying to beat the system. The Army was attempting to teach us discipline, how to wear and care for uniforms, to march in formation, and to have some appreciation of regular army strategy and mission.

There was a saying among the doctors that reflects the general attitude of the drafted Medical Corps, "If you are dishonorably discharged from the service, it looks good on your medical resume".

Basic training actually was fun for most of us. Internships are notorious for low or no pay. The Army paid $2000 a month. As physicians we came in as Captains or Majors, were welcomed at the Officer's Clubs, and had an automatic membership to the golf course on the base. Attending class at the Medical Field Service School was like being on vacation compared to making rounds before 6:00 AM.

It was a month of playing soldier, heavy drinking, and hangovers before many faced the reality of an assignment like Battalion Surgeon in a Vietnam front line jungle outpost.

One week before basic training ended, after hearing another boring lecture the instructor mentioned that a position had opened for an instructor at the Medical Field Service School and anyone who might be interested should stay after class. He said, "class dismissed" and not a person moved.

As I remember we were required to submit some background information and write an essay. To my surprise, I ended up being one of the ten finalists for the position. There was a "teach off" where we were required to teach a mock course in front of several Generals and Bird-Colonel judges. I was able to hear most of the other presentations and judged myself to be about number four.

I left disappointed but not surprised. The next day all doctor draftees were taken to Camp Bullis where we would go through an obstacle course. We were to crawl under live machine gun fire, experience-simulated incoming artillery as explosives in pits were set off as we crawled, were gassed and other out-of-our comfort zone army experiences.

While I was in the middle of this program, a jeep with two enlisted soldiers came to a screeching halt and the driver jumped out calling for Captain Myers. One thing it is important to remember: If someone calls your name while you are crawling under live machine gun fire, NEVER stand up. I didn't but they stopped the guns as a precautionary measure.

The driver said I was ordered immediately to accompany them back to the Medical Field Service School. I scrambled in the jeep and we rapidly drove the 30 miles back to San Antonio. They escorted me to an upstairs office and I was greeted by my soon to be commanding officer, Lt. Colonel John Whitten, who with a big grin shook my hand and said, "Welcome to our team Danny."

In that moment I realized the key to my selection. The only people who called me "Danny" were those who knew me from playing football at Texas. John Whitten was a dyed-in-the-wool Texas football fan.

When my orders were officially changed Yvonne and I purchased a small house off base. I assumed the seller's note as did the guy who bought the house from me two years later. No telling how many people have owned it since that time. For a while I worried that someone would default and the house would come back to me. Fifty years hence, it doesn't look like it is going to happen.

Captain Dan Myers with daughter's Simone and Yvette.
(Belen born toward end of Army service.) Myers family
living in San Antonio while Dan teaching at Medical
Field Service School

What a fortunate, blessed turn of events. I am embarrassed
to admit it never occurred to me to thank God for letting me serve
two years in the service at Ft Sam Houston rather than as a battalion surgeon on the front line in the jungles of Vietnam.

There were three other instructors working in our department, all Captains who had just finished their internships. Initially we were somewhat busy writing lesson plans for courses we would soon be teaching. All Army personnel serving in any medical capacity received their orientation and/or training at the Medical Field Service School. This included physicians, dentists, nurses, physical therapists, corpsmen, hospital administrators, and medical record clerks.

The course that I taught most frequently was "medical terminology." Not exactly an intellectual challenge. In addition, the doctor/instructors took sick call one morning a week. Our patients were mainly high-ranking officers and their families

We also were assigned a role in staged presentations of scenarios of medical response to nuclear attack. Busloads of VIP visitors would be taken to a stadium built in a desolate area of the Texas Hill Country. A major would be standing on the 50 yard line speaking to the crowd about various mundane military issues when he would answer a phone, get a startled expression on his face, and with amazing sincerity say he has just been notified that the United States has just come under attack by an unknown enemy.

Before the audience can appreciate that he must be kidding, a jet aircraft flying near the speed of sound passed several feet above the stadium causing shock and awe. Seconds later about 5 miles away there is a loud explosion producing a mushroom shape cloud. The major shakes his head, announces we have taken a nuclear hit and instructs the audience to load back into the busses as they will be going to access the damage.

When the audience arrives near ground zero they see carnage. There are military vehicles on fire with groaning causalities scattered throughout the wreckage. Corpsmen are rushing about putting on tourniquets on some who have limbs blown off and are bleeding profusely. Moulage and soldier acting had simulated a full array of blast devastation. My role was to be the doctor in the triage tent of a Mobile Army Surgery Hospital (MASH). I would perform some emergency treatment but mainly would sort the salvageable from the dying and direct them toward the appropriate treatment group.

For the actors it was a welcome diversion from their usual military job. One area where, from my perspective, things could get out of hand was in managing psychiatric causalities. Sometimes enlisted men, possibly fed up with an overbearing officer would use the occasion of being assigned the role of psychiatric causality to take a swing at me or one of the other officers.

We discovered the perfect antidote. Evacuation by helicopter would be ordered. For these demonstrations only the small "bubble looking" choppers were used. The only way to evacuate a patient was to strap them on a stretcher tied to one of the pontoons. It turned out to be the perfect cure for feigned post traumatic stress disorder.

The biggest adjustment for most physician/instructors working at the Medical Field Service School was having so little to do. When several groups would be scheduled for orientation at the same time, all five instructors might be needed to teach. However, most of the time there would be only about ten or 15 classes needing a physician instructor in a week. This meant we were only teaching 5-10 hours a week and there were weeks when no groups were scheduled so no classes needed to be taught.

I tried to volunteer at Brooke Army Hospital. Brooke was located at Ft Sam Houston and regularly received severely wounded patients from Vietnam. It was the primary Army treatment hospital for soldiers who had been severely burned.

I had friends there who were working 10 -12 hours a day. For some reason volunteering to help out at Brooke Army Hospital was against Army policy. I also tried moonlighting at local emergency rooms. Turned out the Bexar County Medical Association had an agreement with the Army that no military medical personnel would be permitted to work in a civilian capacity.

After 4 years of medical school and one year of internship when I had seldom been home, two years in the Army with nothing much to do was a big adjustment. I handled it by playing like the Army was summer camp and spent my days and some nights seeing how many ways I could take full advantage of the system.

Yvonne handled it by loading the girls into the car and heading back to Dallas.

I took flying lessons through an Army flying club. Passing ground school was easy. Flying was a different matter. I never became confident or comfortable with myself as the pilot. Stop and go landings particularly were a problem. – I never wanted to go.

I soloed after 12 hours but did not get much encouragement from air traffic control. Our landing strip and hangar was at San Antonio International, which even in 1963 was a busy jet way. I remember coming in to land on designated runway number 90 hearing the traffic controller speak to an American Airlines pilot waiting for take off. "American Bravo 230, advise caution on runway 90. We have a student on 90 doing stop and goes – and I do mean student!" That was one of the days I didn't go. I took a quick right turn and went directly to the hangar.

The last time I flew was after an attempt at a required cross-country trip. The student prepares and files a flight plan for a trip that has three legs. At the end of each leg he lands, gets someone at the airport to sign his logbook, takes off and then does the same for the other leg and then returns home.

As I began my trip I did the required walk around inspection of the plane, a Piper Cub, then checked and topped off the gas tank. I took off but after about 15 minutes saw one little dark cloud so I returned to the airport thinking I would complete this last cross-country on a clearer day.

After landing, my return-trip check-out revealed I hadn't put the gas cap on tight enough, it had blown open and during my short trip almost all the gasoline had blown out. Had I not returned to the airport when I did, I would have had to make an emergency landing.

The experience convinced me that flying is not a safe activity for someone who tends to be distractible, and dislikes attention to detail. In its place, I took up something much safer but that I do even worse, golf.

I next became obsessed with the low prices at the base commissary. I became a butcher. I determined the best bargain was a rib roast. Each week I would cut a couple of roasts into rib eye steaks, beef ribs and flank steak or hamburger. Most of my health problems have been related to some form of arteriosclerosis. I feel sure they were largely caused by my time in the army.

The four MD instructors got along well and we enjoyed being together. However there was one who was equally as hyper and ready for adventure as myself. His name was Jack Harrison. He was married and had two daughters about the same age as Simone and Yvette. Our wives had similar problems. They had husbands who wore them out and after a while they needed rest from them. As you might imagine, Jack and I became great friends.

We spent two years keeping each other on the edge of trouble. We competed almost 24 hours a day. When not working, we hung out at the golf club, drinking beer, playing golf, gin rummy, and chess. We bet on all three and kept a running ledger on how much we owed each other.

Administrative Leave

Six months into the Army I discovered a fantastic source of power. I went to the base library and began to read army regulations. I discovered that, if I was not scheduled for work, I was eligible for administrative leave.

To better implement this plan, I got what was called a Tiger Card. This was obtained through an Air Force program that qualified military personnel to ride as a passenger in a military fighter plane. Examples of the curriculum included learning how to eject from a jet aircraft. This was done in a mock cockpit from which a track ran upward into the air about 30 feet. The seat had an explosive device under it. When the red ejection button was pushed, there was a loud explosion and you and your seat were blown 30 feet up the track. It was critical that you be sitting firmly in your seat when the eject button was pressed. We were told that if there was any space between your rear and the seat, it could break your pelvis.

Another task was being taken up in a high altitude chamber and experiencing and learning to react to loss of cabin pressure. This produced a sudden loud switching noise and the cockpit filled with a cold moist vapor. Before pressure loss occurred we were warned to keep our mouthes partially open so the rapid expansion of the air in our lungs and stomach could rush out. They said if we didn't we might explode. There was nothing said about what might happen to colon gas.

After putting on oxygen masks we were taken to a higher altitude and told to remove them so that we could experience and learn to recognize the effect of oxygen loss. It was a surprise to learn there was no sense of air hunger. Instead there was a subtle, and gradual loss of orientation, coordination and eventually consciousness. As we began to black out, instructors replaced our oxygen masks. Learning to escape from a ditched plane was practiced in a swimming pool.

There were three Air Force Bases around San Antonio; and I made the most of space-available travel. Doctors were particularly welcome on military aircraft. We were thought of as nice insurance to have on board in case of a medical emergency, but more often it was a convenient time for the crew to get medical advice and treatment for minor ailments.

During my two years in the Army, I flew space-available to Disneyland in Los Angeles, the World's Fair in New York City, Costa Rica to see a friend working with the Peace Corps, to Panama City, Panama, Quito, Ecuador, and Guatemala. The trip to Guatemala was in an old, loud DC 3. I was the only passenger. Shortly after takeoff I noticed the pilot and copilot were wearing parachutes. I asked if they had another one and they found one which I wore the rest of the trip.

I once caught a flight in a Lear jet carrying a general to a meeting in Seattle. Also, Yvonne and I traveled through Europe space-available.

Our Europe trip occurred about two months after our third daughter, Belen was born. Belen's birth was an example of another Army opportunity. Because of the rumors about less than optimum Army obstetric care, I made another trip to the library and learned about a regulation permitting an officer's wife to have private medical care if she was residing in another city.

Several weeks before Belen was due Yvonne and the girls moved in with my parents in Waco, Texas so that she could be cared for by Dr. Tom Husbands, a respected Waco obstetrician and family friend.

Since everyone seemed to have gotten along so great in Waco, my parents agreed to keep the children while Yvonne and I tried to get to Europe space-available. In mid-December 1964 we went to Lackland Air Force Base and checked to see if there was a flight going to London, our first choice. There was not; but there was a plane leaving for Scotland. That was fine for us so we got on. The plane was a prop plane, all the seats were facing backwards and it was filled with women and children, dependents of army personnel.

Sitting next to me was a woman who appeared to be in the mist of a manic episode of a bipolar disorder. For 12 hours she exhausted us, and others, with her wild grandiose ravings. When we landed in Greenland to refuel (we were only half way to Europe because it was a prop plane and there was a strong headwind), I knew we couldn't stand another 12 hours of her ravings. I got off the plane, arranged for an army vehicle to take me to their dispensary where I picked up a bottle of large dose thorazine capsules. She accepted the, "trust me I am a doctor line" and agreed to swallow several. The silence that prevailed was so appreciated that I was surprised that I was not recommended for a medal.

Twelve hours later we were on final approach to Edinburg when the copilot came back to my seat and said, "Captain Myers" (turns out I was the highest ranking officer on the plane), I am sorry but the Edinburg ceiling will not permit us to land so we are proceeding to London." That was fine with us as that was where we had originally hoped to go. The problem was that three hours later, the pilot returned and said, Captain Myers, London is socked in, we are diverting to Frankfort." Germany had been on our planned itinerary so that was OK also.

About two hours later, he returned to say, "Captain Myers, we can not land in Frankfurt, we are going to try to make it to France." To which I said, "Lieutenant. please land this plane at the nearest safe place. I do not want you to again notify me of destinations any place in between." Two hour later, flying on fumes, we landed in Chateaux, France, only a few miles outside of Paris.

In a little over a two week period we visited France, Germany, Switzerland, Belgium, England, and Spain. Most of it was by space-available travel. Many places we were able to spend the night at officers' quarters on an airbase. The next morning we would have breakfast, then check the chalkboard postings to see where flights were going that day. If we had not been there, we usually got on a flight. The only requirement was flexibility and stamina, two of my strong suits. Yvonne was young and I had not had not worn her out yet. We had a great time!

Although most doctors would have preferred not being drafted, and most did what they could to soften the circumstances of their two-year commitment, I never knew one who fled to Canada to escape their military obligation. Although they exhibited a MASH-like persona, they were patriotic and would have served as ordered. All doctor-instructors at the Medical Field Service School had a secondary assignment to a STRIKE unit and could be called to Vietnam at any time. Our laissez faire attitude was regularly curtailed by a rumor that our STRIKE unit was about to be deployed. Even though I make light of it, I feel privileged and proud to have served in the military.

Psychiatry Residency

By the time my Army commitment was served, my interest in psychiatry had waned. However, acceptance into a residency program at Timberlawn Psychiatric Center in Dallas was a convenient transition from Army life back into the "real medical world". Yvonne was back in her hometown where she had her high school friends and parents. I figured that one year of psychiatry, regardless of what residency I eventually pursued, couldn't hurt me. The pay for a private hospital psychiatry residency was good and Timberlawn provided housing and meals for the resident and family.

At the time it seemed like a very reasonable decision. However, in retrospect, there were better choices than having your family live in a mental hospital. We did it for six months before Yvonne's parents loaned us the money to make a down payment on a home in the Park Cities.

Once I started the psychiatry residency I was hooked and I have never regretted my choice. The practice of psychiatry allows for a quality of life hard to match in other areas of medicine. It encourages broader interests than just medicine. My experience has been that having a child psychiatrist in a family is a useful luxury. The number of calls I receive from parents in our extended family and from parents of friends seems significantly higher than the amount received in other specialties. Some might consider this a disadvantage. For me it seems a blessing. What greater pleasure is there than helping those you care so much about. Another bonus is being able to correct two common myths of the general public that psychiatrists are crazier than their patients, and that all psychiatrists are atheists.

Timberlawn, in the 1960's, was one of the premier training centers for psychiatrists in the US. It was a private psychiatric hospital with a long standing tradition. During the time when I was doing my residency it was flushed with success and money. Timberlawn drew wealthy patients from all over the country. In those days, insurance companies prided themselves in carrying health insurance that covered mental illness. Although the senior staff were well paid, a significant of the hospital income was used for research, and the training of psychiatric residents.

During my residency training, 1965 to 1969, the average hospital stay for an adolescent was eighteen months. From 1970 through the next 50 years insurance companies continually decreased the benefits paid for treating mental illness. By 2015 the average hospital stay had dropped from 540 days to 4.5 days. During the transition there was gradual deterioration of mental health services through out the nation. The psychiatric residency and research at Timberlawn could not be supported and were discontinued. Long standing staff positions were lost and there was increasing staff turn over. By 2015 Timberlawn declared bankruptcy and began to have difficulty with accreditation as well as multiple law suits. How fortunate, blessed? I was to have been trained at Timberlawn during its golden period.

Similar to the first day of my internship, my first morning of psychiatry residency was eventful. I was assigned as the staff doctor for a 21 year old female drug addict who had been admitted the previous night. As I entered the female unit, she walked toward me to introduce herself and on the way had a gran mal seizure, falling to the floor bleeding and unconscious from hitting her head on a piece of furniture. Psychiatrists are also trained in neurology. I had not expected to need it so soon.

The theoretical bias for teaching at Timberlawn was psychoanalytic. Residents read the works of Sigmund Freud, Carl Jung and others. We were taught to look for the unconscious conflicts and motivations of patients' behavior, and to formulated our cases using psychodynamics. Concepts such as castration anxiety, narcissism, separation anxiety, penis envy, panic attacks, sibling rivalry, were part of our regular thought processes as our professors attempted to open our minds to the mystery and darkness of the unconscious human mind.

I remember trying to explain some of things I was learning to my father. Rosy's only comment was, "Damn Dan, you picked one Hell of a career!" The rumination (another psychiatric concept) described above are a prelude that I hope the reader will take into consideration before too harshly judging three psychiatry resident friends and myself. If you don't, you may jump to the conclusion that the is just another example of how nutty psychiatrists can be.The following is a story of a mutual illusion and embarrassing experience that I have never before admitted:

During our psychiatry residency, three other residents, Dr. Doyle Carson, Dr. Frank Crumley, Dr. Taft Moore and myself, developed the routine of playing two-on-two touch football games Sunday afternoons at Caruth Park in Dallas. The physical exercise was an excellent diversion from the bizarre psychoanalytic concepts we were immersed in during the workweek.

One afternoon I chased an overthrown football into a flowerbed and stopped dead in my tracts. Turn the page. You are not going to believe what I found!!!

Stinkhorns are astonishing. Their abrupt appearance in gardens and lawns is frequently the cause of considerable consternation; they arise from an "egg" that results from the immature mushroom's universal veil, quickly breaking the "shell" and thrusting themselves up to heights of nearly 10 inches in a matter of hours!

Phallus impudicus covers its tip with a foul smelling and spore-laden slime; flies are attracted to it, and carry the spores away as they continue on their little fly adventures

I called the others over to see my discovery. Our minds, fresh from hearing case histories of psychotic patients who castrated themselves or others, unanimously concluded we had discovered a heinous crime scene. We got sticks and dug around expecting to find other body parts. Inside what appeared to be the scrotum was a Vaseline appearing substance. Each sack seemed to hold a testicle. The odor was foul. Flies buzzed around the material. We cordoned off the area and warned parents walking by in the park to keep their children away from the dig site. Doyle goes (no cell phones then) to call the police.

The University Park police come. Accepting the conclusion of four physicians, they get a shovel, dig, find no other sign of a body, put the specimen carefully in a plastic bag, take our names, and head to Parkland Hospital and their pathology department. We are assured they will follow up with us as the case develops.

We all agree that it is best not to discuss the matter with anyone. Such a secret is hard to keep. There was only one person I felt confident of confiding in. This was my supervisor and chairman of the Department of Child Psychiatry, Dr. Jack Martin. Such a supervisor/student relationship is always confidential. Dr. Martin waited anxiously like myself and the other three residents for the pathologist's call

Not having heard anything for a week, I gave him a call. He told me that when he had received the specimen in a plastic bag all that remained was a unrecognizable pile of wilted organic matter. Microscopic examination showed it was a mushroom. Horrified, with great trepidation, I placed the call to my supervisor, Jack Martin. Dr. Martin, shared an office complex with a dignified, serious psychologist, Dr Francis Hauk. When Dr. Martin said, "A Mushroom?" I heard a loud thump. I asked, "What was that?" He said, "That was Francis. She just fell to the floor from laughing" - So much for confidentiality.

Assuming we were the laughingstock of the hospital was a certain antidote for taking ourselves too seriously. For years I lived in fear that someday someone would be reviewing the UP police log and publish the story in the Park Cities People. So far, so good.

However, for many years after this supposedly secret event, I received anonymous notes in the mail such as the one below:

Despite our shenanigans, Timberlawn's reputation was not ruined and it continued to be a leading teaching treatment center. We with greater discernment learned the most recent scientific research and modern forms of psychiatric treatment. In addition to psychoanalytic concepts, we were taught the latest advances in psychopharmacology, although fewer medications were available in that era.

Electric and insulin shock were being used regularly for the treatment of severe depression and schizophrenia. First year residents were responsible for administering electric convulsive therapy and insulin shock each morning. By today's standards it was primitive. No anesthesiologist was present so the resident administered what little anesthesia was given.

We would take a syringe filled with a light sedative and curare and inject the patient intravenously. Curare is a substance that paralyzes muscles, decreasing the likelihood that patients would fracture bones during their seizure. Unfortunately it also paralyzes the diaphragm, resulting in loss of the ability to breathe. As the breathing stopped, paddles were put on each side of the head and electricity discharged. This resulted in the patient having a convulsion and losing consciousness.

We would aerate patients with a breathing bag until they began to breathe on their own, usually two to three minutes. The patient would have no memory of the procedure. How much long term memory was lost was variable. After several weeks memory seemed back to normal for most. However, if the patient received multiple treatments more memory was lost. To what degree this is permanent, is difficult to determine.

Each of the first year residents would do six to eight EST treatments each morning, making us by the end of our first year being some of the most experienced people in America at doing shock treatments. Since shock treatments are seldom used today, we may still hold that distinction.

We also did insulin shock treatments. Even in that time this was more controversial and dangerous. EST was a well-established treatment for severe depression; no one was sure whether insulin shock was actually effective. It was prescribed mostly for paranoid schizophrenics who had not responded to the limited number of antipsychotic drugs that were available. We usually had two or three insulin shock patients to do each morning.

The nurses timed their insulin injections linked to how soon we would be finished with EST. When we arrived at the insulin treatment room the patients would be in bed, restrained by sheets in a mummy-like fashion and usually delirious. Their sheets would be dripping wet with sweat, an early indicator of insulin shock. Often the patient's personality would be regressed and they would seem to be reacting to past events, talking in a younger, infantile voice or in a nonsensical manner.

We would watch the patients closely and speak reassuring words so they would be less frightened by the experience. I could have used some reassuring words myself. It was a dangerous assignment. We had been taught the signs for judging the depth of the patient's coma: perspiring, shivering, pupil dilatation, loss of rational consciousness, loss of corneal reflex (not blinking when the eye was touched with a whist of cotton), loss of deep tendon reflexes, failure to respond to pain, seizure, and if the coma continued, death.

My first insulin coma patient is vividly remembered. I came into the treatment room mildly hung over from the continuation of a US Army drinking pattern. When the correct level of coma was achieved, the coma is ended by injecting intravenous glucose. As the glucose is injected the patient slowly regains consciousness. The needle used is large gauge as the glucose is thick and syrup-like. The location and successful threading of a vein with the large needle and syringe filled with glucose can be a tense situation, particularly with an inexperienced and slightly hung-over young resident.

I remember the relief I felt as a large vein was located. I penetrated the vein and drew blood back into the syringe to insure that the point of the needle was not outside the vein. Spilling glucose outside of the vein into the surrounding tissue would cause a painful swelling and could provide an area for bacterial growth and infection. What caught me unexpectedly was the sight of the bright red blood billowing, contrasted with the crystal clear glucose, into the syringe like a slowly moving red storm cloud. The sight of it caused me, for the only time in my life, to almost faint. The experience very quickly taught me that I would have to curtail evening alcohol drinking.

After the insulin patient receives the glucose into the vein, consciousness returns and she/he passes into a normal restful sleep. The therapeutic effect of insulin shock is not as dramatic as it is in ECT. It may be weeks or months before a decrease in irrational thinking is observed Although more dangerous, the insulin treatments did not frighten the patient or seem as barbaric as electric shock to the patient or staff. With insulin shock there was no significant memory loss.

Timberlawn was a great learning experience. It was demanding, with emergency workups and calls frequently during the night. However, it was a piece of cake compared to other specialty residencies. Psychiatry residents were paid a livable wage. Being a psychiatrist, most of us were spared having to deal regularly with the death of a patient.

It is said that the specialty of anesthesiology can be days of boring routine, broken by minutes of absolute panic and terror. Psychiatry would usually not be described as boring, but one of the perils of practicing psychiatry is that the routine of many patients having life adjustment problems that respond fairly easily to psychotherapy and or medication can lull the psychiatrist into a false sense of security.

One of my early patients as a psychiatric resident was a pretty young woman who suffered postpartum depression. She was admitted to the hospital in a manic state. For the six months that she was in the hospital I, under the supervision of a senior staff psychiatrist, was her doctor. Her case fascinated me and she was delightful. I saved many of her paintings and poetic writings and used them to decorate my private office after my training.

When I had last seen her, I assumed she was on her way to a well-adjusted and happy life. Several years later I ran into the doctor who had assumed her outpatient care. He told me she had committed suicide by cutting her own throat with an electric carving knife.

The risk of a patient committing suicide must always be on your mind. Teenagers, in particular are at risk for death. Automobile accidents, suicide, drug overdose, homicide, pregnancy, criminal activity, alcoholism, runaways, are a few of the hurdles teens must circumvent to pass through adolescence alive.

Although treating young children usually has the advantage that there are loving parents working faithfully to keep the child safe, there are some families in which the parents are the major problem. In addition, adolescence is a time when children want to be in control of their own destiny so they devalue the good sense guidance their parents are trying to impose. This dynamic, pushing to be independent from parents, proceeds even though science and parental experience has clearly demonstrated that most teenagers have not neurologically matured enough to make regular good judgements.

Early childhood patients are less a worry for death. However even young children can be depression prone. Since young children may not understand the permanency of death, they can present a special risk.

I have evaluated four children who had killed one or both parents. Although most patients we see are interesting, enjoyable, and present minimal risk to themselves and others, psychiatrists must be vigilant. The lesson is clear: Never become bored, complacent, cocky, work under the influence, hungover, or careless, when you are engaged in the mental health field.

At the end of my second year at Timberlawn I decided to add an additional two years of training to become qualified as a child and adolescent psychiatrist as well as an adult psychiatrist. This meant the last two and half years of the five-year program would be done at the Department of Psychiatry, Southwestern Medical School.

Before beginning child psychiatry training, Timberlawn agreed to let me do the last three of my months of my adult residency at the Terrell State Hospital in Terrell, Texas, about 30 minutes east of Dallas. Although this was not a standard part of the training, my view was that a psychiatrist should have some experience at a state mental institution, as this was where treatment failures, the poor, and people who had exhausted all insurance benefits end.

When Timberlawn granted my petition in 1967 to do a three month rotation at the Terrell State Hospital, the superintendent, Dr. Luis Cowley assigned me as the doctor for two chronic patient units, each housing approximately 100 patients.

My rotation began on a cold January morning. This unit was drab and bare and cold enough that most of the patients were wearing several layers of clothing. What startled me was to find many of the patients lying on the floor head to toe in geometric patterns.

The aid explained that what I was seeing was how the plumbing was laid out inside the concrete floors. The patients were lying over the hot water pipes that crisscrossed running through the concrete. Most of the patients had been housed on these units for 15 to 20 years. Many had not seen a doctor for more than five years.

I set up a schedule that allowed me to interview every patient during my three-month rotation. I was determined to discharge a large number of them from the hospital. I did interview every one, but discharged none. Although many could have been managed as outpatients, they had nowhere to go. Their families had forgotten them years ago.

After my three months at Terrell I began my child psychiatry fellowship at UT Southwestern. There is something about treating children and adolescents for me that made it easier to keep my sense of humor. For example, the time a ten year old boy was brought to see me because he had shaved the family long haired dog to look like a lion.

There was also the 14 year boy who was angry at his parents and decided to run away. He rode his bicycle to the train station, got on a freight train and rode it to Ft Worth, about 35 miles west of Dallas. He then decided he had made a mistake and caught another train back. When he was telling me about his trip I expressed my concern about the danger involved. He said he had no problem during the trip and that he especially enjoyed the ride back to Dallas. The train back to Dallas was carrying new cars so he just got in one of them for the ride back. I couldn't help but ask, "what type of cars?" He said all kinds but his was a Ford Pinto.

So I asked him why he didn't ride in a more luxury car? He said it was because somebody was already in those.

The pace of child psychiatry training was not as intense as adult psychiatry had been at Timberlawn and Terrell. I even had time for some hobbies. One that evolved was a preoccupation with"want-ad" shopping - basically a precursor to "Craigslist".

As our family regularly had a need for certain household items this mini obsession sometimes served a useful purpose. My strategy was to get the newspaper early Friday morning and find the newly classified for-sale items. If something was interesting I would try to be the first one at the location when it opened for business. I found some unbelievable bargains! This hobby started with buying a breakfast room table and chairs. After the breakfast-furniture passion, came a fixation on car luggage carriers, then electric lawnmowers, playground equipment, bicycles, sailboats, houseboats, and my most ambitious endeavor, buying a lake house.

Several years previous, I had invested $5,000 with my father to complete a house he was building for my grandmother. When my dad sold the house after her death he returned the $5,000 plus my portion of the profit that was another $5,000. This gave me $10,000, more cash than I had ever had in a bank.

The money would be used for a down payment on a lake house. I started in earnest to apply my Dallas Morning News classified skills to the real estate section. Two weeks went by and nothing affordable showed up. Then on a Friday morning, the third week of my search, an advertisement came up that I could not believe. It said "For Sale: Lake house on Lake Tawakoni, $10,000. Open house tours Saturday and Sunday." The address was given, but no telephone number. I got up at 5:00 AM Saturday and headed to Lake Tawakoni, about 70 miles southeast of Dallas. The sun was just coming up when I arrived at what appeared to be a fishing cabin, painted barn red with a smoke stack gently puffing out smoke. The lot was high in grass and weeds. I knocked on the door and an older man opened it and invited me inside. He was sitting at a kitchen table drinking coffee. The house consisted of one large room, a bathroom and a kitchen. Hanging from the walls were various stuffed ducks, a deer head and the head mount of a large black bear. I asked him the price of the house and he said $10,000.

I said, "for the down payment?" He answered, "No, the house." I said, "I'll take it," and he said "fine." He found a paper sack on a shelf and drew up a contact. I gave him a $1000 check as a down payment and he wrote out the name of a title company he uses. After shaking hands on the deal, he gave me the keys and started to walk out the door. I asked where he was going. He said, "The house is yours. I am going back to Dallas." All his furniture, his plates, glasses and silverware, his coffee pot still brewing, his mounted animals were left with me. I had bought a house for $10,000. When the lot was cleared, I discovered it was 1-½ acres of land. I built a screened in sleeping porch across the back of the house and rented 30% interest to two close friends. I bought a 16 foot Hobie catamaran sailboat (also through the want ads) and installed a transom that would accept a 20 horsepower motor. Quick release clamps were found that enabled the mast to be quickly removed. If the wind was not good, we would take off the mast and sails, and could ski, tube, or fish. It was great family fun for about 10 years. The fun ended when each of all three men's wives divorced them.

I decided to sell the lake house and took my boat out for one last time before I ran my ad in *The Dallas Morning News*. That day there was no wind so I ditched sails and put on the motor and went fishing. Although in the ten years I had used the boat, I had never seen a game warden, that last day one pulled up beside me. He was not impressed with my Hobie Cat/motorboat adaptation. I received citations for not being registered as a motor boat, not having enough life vests, carrying no fire extinguisher, and not having a fishing license.

I wrote my ad that night and it read "Lake house for sale at Lake Tawakoni. Includes Hobie Cat sailboat with trailer, $20,000. Open Saturday and Sunday." I spent Friday night there and was drinking coffee when there was knock on the door about 6:45AM. A young man came in and asked the price for the house. I said $20,000. He said "$20,000 - total?" When I nodded he quickly said "I want it! I drew up a contract on notepaper, got a deposit, gave him the keys and the name of a title company I used and started out the door. He said, "Wait. What about all these things?" I shrugged my shoulders, got in the car and drove back to Dallas. That is last I saw of him or the house. I believe I could have sold it for about $30,000 or more; It just was too satisfying to sell it the same way I bought it.

There is one more story I want to tell about the lake house. Not long after I bought it, I began to hatch an idea about planning a family cross country bicycle ride from our house in Dallas, 70 miles away. I had a large, heavy black three speed Raleigh English bike (bought through a want ad) that I was eager to take on the road. As you can imagine, no family member, certainly not my wife, was interested. Their wisdom prevailed so I decided I should not impose this family trip on them until I had tried it myself.

One Sunday in early September about 4:00 in the morning I started out to Lake Tawakoni The carrot I was using to encourage me onward was that the Cowboy game was blacked out in Dallas but I would be able to watch it at the lake house. By noon it was 100 degrees and I was facing a strong headwind. The road had become narrow and I periodically would be almost run off the road by pick-ups. I fantasized that some would begin throwing beer cans at me as they passed. I took comfort in the fact that in the handlebar basket, under a towel and some water was a loaded 38. Obviously, even to me, this trip would never do for a family outing. I stopped at a gas station to get a cold drink and contemplated the last hour and one half I had to go.

Suddenly, a terrible thought popped into my head. I remembered that the last time we were at the lake house we had taken the TV back to Dallas with us. I used some change to call Yvonne to see if she would bring the TV to the lake. I had to listen again to what a harebrained idea this had been but I eventually got her to agree to come. I got back on my bike and continued on my ordeal. I had just pulled into the entrance to the division where our house was about 3 blocks away when Yvonne drove up in our station wagon.

She rolled down the window and said, "there is room in the back, put your bike in the car." I was dumbfounded! "Does she think I am going to ride 70 miles and then put my bike in the car for the last two blocks?" She shook her head in exasperation and drove on to the house. In retrospect I realize I was fortunate she didn't turn the car around and drive back to Dallas with the TV.

The house Yvonne's parents had helped us buy was on Caruth Blvd. in University Park. After living several years there, the real estate market was so hot that I convinced Yvonne to sell the house for a considerable profit and buy a larger house on an oversized lot on Beverly Drive in Highland Park.

I had finished my adult psychiatry residency at Timberlawn, and was beginning the Child Psychiatry Fellowship at the medical school. It was not completely an accident that the Beverly house I wanted to buy was next door to the residence of Dr. Jack Martin, the Chairman of the Department of Child Psychiatry at UT Southwestern Medical School. We became close friends and he became godfather to Dan Jr.

Reflections on College Age Period

A National Institute of Mental Health Publication, No. 11-4929 reports research showing that the teenage brain is still undergoing neurologic development during the teenage years and does not reach normal adult neurologic maturity until the mid twenties. This postulates that the clinical findings of adolescents' high impulsivity, risk taking , binge drinking and sleep abnormalities may be related to brain immaturity. Psychological testing shows that dangerous risk taking of adolescents also significantly increases when in the company of like-minded peers.

Parents, looking back on their own childhood, often assume that their children experience leaving home similar to the way they did. Things are very different. Many theologians refer to the current age as "post-christian." A post-christian world is one in which Christianity and its teachings are no longer dominant. Parents can not anticipate that the people who are significant to the college age child will have values filtered through generations of relatives trusting in the Bible's wisdom. Christian thinking and values are now in the minority.

Colleges pride themselves in treating students like adults. To me they seem intimidated by the students. They discourage and impede parents from exercising control in the students' lives. Hovering "Helicopter Parents" are objects of scorn. Parental "hovering" can have various motivations. It is a bad thing when parents hover to relive their own fantasy about college life or are over-invested in their child's social life; it is another to be stymied by colleges not allowing parents to know if their children have attended class or that they have failed their courses. Treating college students like adults when they act like children can be dangerous. During "the good old days" when the parents were in college there were rules such as dorm curfews, not having others sleep over in your room, enforced no alcohol or smoking rules, and many other regulations consistent with the students' maturity, - or lack there of. My view is that college deans lead the way in being overindulgent, permissive, and giving in to the whims of entitled, immature, unrealistic students. There is no question that "children or colleges are not like they use to be"

Reviewing my college age foolishness and risky behavior from "the good old days" doesn't seem to be a good model for anyone. However, providing more relief from authority certainly would not be an answer.

In my day there were college age young people who seemed to have their "head on straight." These students maintained an internal moral compass. Mostly they were "church people." At the time none of them were my close friends. I ran with a different group. Although I passed through this dangerous period relatively unscathed, looking back I feel I was pressing my luck. Suicides, accident deaths, and criminal activity are much higher during college age.

Rick Warren in his bestseller book, <u>The Purpose Driven Life</u>, warns of the shortness of our life on earth compared to eternal life in Heaven. Leaving home for college having already internalized Christian values and continuing to have the reenforcement of regular Church attendance may provide protection that would have eternal consequences. Associating with other college age Christians should be supportive. Parents can encourage all this by helping their student to locate a Church and attending Church with him/her when visiting them at college.

Young Adult Stage

By stacking my required course work and clinical service during the first one and one half years of the child psychiatric residency I managed to have the last six months as electives. This allowed time to prepare for entering the private practice of Dallas psychiatry. Having had rotations working and training at Timberlawn Psychiatric Center, the Dallas Child Guidance Clinic, the Terrell State Hospital The Denton State School, consulting with the Highland Park and Dallas School Districts, the Salesmanship Camp, and there being a shortage of child psychiatrists, I was well positioned to receive referrals. By June 1969 when the residency officially ended, I was seeing enough private patients to have an a full schedule should I decide to open a private practice.

The dilemma was whether to join admired professors at Southwestern Medical School or Timberlawn Psychiatric Center and enjoy the status and perks of being associated with an established teaching program, or take the risk and presumed loss of prestige of starting a private practice. My decision was a compromise. Rather than to prioritize making money, I decided I would provide as many of the perks associated with academic psychiatry as possible while still doing private practice. This meant there would be less profit but more quality of life, without having to be a salaried employee. After I identified the specific features of academic practice that I coveted it surprised me how easy it was to build them into a private practice.

For example, medical school staff are given time off and expenses to attend a national psychiatry meeting each year. All I had to do was take off the time and pay my own way to whatever meetings I wanted to attend. Although I would lose income during the absence, annual profit would still be greater than an academic salary. A renowned child psychoanalyst, Dr. Robert Long, at the medical school conducted a weekly conference the psychiatry faculty could attend. I hired him as a consultant and invited those psychiatrists who I wished to attend to come to my office once a week for a conference. I also hired the Child Psychiatry Department's administrative secretary and best social worker to join me in private practice.

Rather than rent an office, I bought a small house on Lovers Lane in Dallas close to Highland Park High School and the Shelton School, a school for children with learning differences. The house provided the privacy and space required to conduct both child and adolescent therapy groups, a feature available in no other Dallas private practice of child psychiatry. It also provided a comfortable, non-intimidating atmosphere for seeing child patients and their parents. In addition, I was invited to join the clinical faculty of the department of psychiatry at Southwestern, achieving the rank of Associate Professor.

The practice quickly expanded. The house next door to my office happened to be a mirror image of the one I owned so I purchased it and joined the two together with a large waiting room. This provided office and parking space that housed three child psychiatrists, a PhD psychologist, and a LPC family therapist. The Myers Psychiatry Clinic was born.

It was during this period that the Dallas Salesmanship Camp was having great success using a wilderness camp as an alternative to hospitalization for disturbed adolescents. Using my GI bill, and partnering with two other child psychiatrists (both had previously been UT Southwestern Child Psychiatry Chairmen) we purchased 200 acres of East Texas wilderness. We built a nice lake and stocked it with fish. Garden Valley Wilderness Camp was very quickly ready for business. The only token given to civilization at the camp was a telephone line going to a phone hidden under a log. The concept was that campers would build their own living sites, plan and cook their own meals, and use the collective process of survival to learn relational skills and the fundamentals of education. The wilderness would be able to teach reality testing and promote problem solving in a uniquely nonjudgmental fashion. For example, if a camper did not build his shelter rain proof, it did not mean he was a bad person or that the staff didn't like him; it just meant he was going to get wet.

The Dallas Salesmanship Camp had data showing that after a wilderness treatment program, troubled adolescents were able to return to school at the same grade level as their peers who had been in a traditional education setting. The Dallas Independent

School District credited Wilderness Camp experience the same as if the teens had been in regular school.

Primarily because of the academic stature of the two other psychiatrists, our camp was accredited by the joint commission of hospitals, despite us not having a single permanent structure on the property. More amazing was that the Joint Commission inspection of Garden Valley Wilderness Camp happened to occur during a severe ice storm.

As the Camp's Medical Director, I was primarily responsible for developing the treatment program and hiring, training, and supervising staff. We advertised in the Dallas Morning News classified section, explaining that mental health staff would live and work with disturbed adolescents in a wilderness setting in East Texas under the supervision of child psychiatrists. Salary would be dependent on qualifications. None of us anticipated the response. I expected we might have no applicants. We had over a hundred qualified respondents..

We eventually selected two male 28-year-old PhD psychologists who arrived for their interview in a Volkswagen bus with a canoe strapped on top. Both seemed exceptionally stable and suited as ego ideals for teen-age boys. One, of the two, had been the youngest director in the United States of a Boy Scout Camp.

The joint owners of the camp consisted of three child psychiatrists and one family therapist social worker. We were all board certified, active in academic psychiatry as well as having a private practice, and were good friends. We had six teenage male patients who we felt were good candidates for wilderness camping treatment, and their parents were eagerly awaiting for us to open.

As a crucial part of the camp program was that the campers, with the supervision of the two counselors ,would build their own shelters and other facilities, no construction needed to be arranged by the owners. In several weeks we were ready for the six campers and Garden Valley Wilderness Camp was up and running.

From the onset we were seeing positive change and therapeutic result in our campers. I and the two other owner/psychiatrists would regularly go to the camp and meet with campers and the two counselors to provide supervision and support.

We would discuss the conflicts and dynamics of the camp. Most issues were resolved easier than we had seen in more traditional treatment facilities, and the boys were happy camping out and not having to go to regular school.

Our counselors lived with the boys for six months with no time off, some of it during a severe winter. How they did it I never understood. They were the most dedicated, conscientious, toughest, and determined young men on the planet. They shaped six hyperactive, authority-hating hellions into a cohesive, functional group, that not only lived through a harsh wilderness environment but thrived in it.

Only once did the counselors diverge from their path of sacrificial support to arrange a modicum of pleasure for themselves. They used the log phone to invite their girlfriends to drive down to visit the camp. They introduced the girlfriends to the campers and then the two couples took a stroll around the lake. While they were walking the campers stole the girls' car and proceeded on a wild joy ride. None of the six were old enough to have a license. That night they were stopped and arrested in a small east Texas town about 60 miles from the camp.

I never got the complete story on how the car theft/elopement was handled. I am confident the counselors turned it into a learning experience for the hoodlum patients. I can tell you how it ended. One day in late spring, there was a knock on my Dallas office door. I opened it to find the Chief counselor. He walked into my office, looked me in the eye and said, "Doctor Myers, I have come to realize that all of my life I have made every effort to stay away from the type of people I am now living with. I quit!" He walked out, got into his Volkswagen bus with the canoe on top and rode into the sunset. His partner soon followed suit.

I never heard from either of the counselors again. The campers returned to their families and the parents were amazed at how they had matured. Garden Valley Wilderness closed and we owners congratulated themselves that we hadn't lost any money, and had not been sued. I ended up with a 100 acre farm, mineral rights and one of the best fishing lakes in the county.

Several years after we shut down the Garden Valley Wilderness camp, the Salesmanship Program also closed as did many other wilderness programs in the country. It turned out that the research reporting of such positive results had been flawed and insurance coverage became more difficult to obtain. As far as we know, our boys continued to do well.

The Myers Child and Adolescent Clinic also gave up the ghost. This statement could sum up its course, "My practice was great, but my business was bad!" I was immature and did not have the experience to manage such a growing and complex organization. The most fundamentals mistake made was paying the professional staff a percentage of what they billed, not what was collected. Everyone was doing great financially except me.

Seeing the patients myself could be done with much less overhead, fewer headaches, and more profit. I closed the Clinic. The professionals associated with me were exceptionally capable and none had difficulty transitioning into another rewarding position. The staff gradually moved out of my office building and I resumed the active solo practice of child psychiatry.

Shortly after the staff had relocated, an exciting real estate opportunity presented itself. The Mount Zion Baptist Church located at 5120 McKinney had been bought by a group of attorneys. They had planned to tear the church down and build a new office building. They changed their mind and put the property up for sale. The property was divided into two lots, one had the Church on it, the other was the parking lot for the Church. Both were for sale. The church lot was $1000 more than the parking lot. I sold my clinic office to another child psychiatrist and bought the lot with the church on it, essentially paying only $1,000 for a 6000 square ft building. It was in 1975, a year when the economy was booming. An interim loan was obtained for construction.

The construction loan had a deadline for when the building must be completed and then permanent financing would be put in place. Early in the project it became obvious that construction was going too slow to make the deadline. In a restoration, problems are regularly uncovered that are unexpected. By the time the contractor would reach me and I would make a decision on what should be done, days would be wasted. For me, it was a desperate situation. The economy had cooled by this time and banks were eager to get out of loans such as mine. If I did not meet the deadline I felt certain I would lose the building and the money I had already invested.

The remedy I devised was to schedule my patients only in the afternoon and every morning I showed up at the job site in work clothes, a nail apron and gloves. I worked side by side with the construction crews. Decisions were made instantly, the workmen began to appreciate my dilemma and everyone's effort increased. When the date for inspection was two days away everything was finished except some painting. Thankfully a group of friends joined me for those two days and together we finished the project and permanent financing was secured. What had been the Sunday school was developed into an elementary school for children with learning and emotional problems. It was named, "The Old Church School." The sanctuary became 3 office units and a waiting room.

About this same time my father, Rosy Myers developed serious health and financial problems. I drove to Kerrville where he and my mother were living. He was close to death from emphysema, malignant hypertension, and congestive heart failure. I drove my parents back to Dallas and admitted my father to Parkland hospital under the care of my friend, thoracic surgeon, Dr. Bill Snyder. Dr Snyder operated on Rosy, removing a horseshoe kidney that was causing his hypertension, and replaced his abdominal aorta, renal and femoral arteries. He saved Rosy's life and gave him back to me in better health than he had been in twenty years.

We remodeled an unused portion of the church building to make my parents an apartment. He was an experienced businessman, having owned a construction and real estate company. Business guidance was sorely needed and he was a big help. He also guided me into real estate ventures that turned out profitable for us both.

One day Rosy and I noticed that a "For Sale" sign had gone up on the lot behind my building. The lot faced on Central Expressway and was very desirous for us as it gave us frontage on both McKinney Avenue and Central Expressway. I asked Rosy to look into it. Rosy negotiated a good price and secured 100%financing from a local bank. After purchasing the lot we discovered there was an advertising sign on it that faced Central Expressway.

The sign was leased and the fees from the rental were now payable to me. It turned out that the rental income was exactly the amount of the repayment schedule of my 100% loan.

The building continued to be a lifetime blessing. When Yvonne's and my divorce was eminent, the building asset was put into an educational trust for our children. Subsequently I sold the building for a profit and carried the entire note at 18% interest only. This interest paid for college for our four children and when the note finally came due in full, Yvonne and I split the amount of the original sale price.

In my later years during the time when my father worked with me as a business manager we developed a close, respectful meaningful father/son relationship. I came to understand early family relationships that made me realize my childhood and adolescent views toward my father were often inaccurate and unfair.

There is another colorful story about the Church building. Several years after the building was sold, the attorney who purchased the building was having a drink with a business associate in what had been my office. An argument ensued that ended in a gunfight. The owner killed his associate and got off on self-defense. He later sold the building to another person who was subject to my same note. Rosy had drawn up the note with no prepayment privilege.

My father, Rosy Myers, me wearing a toupee and Dan Jr. standing in front of the remodeled Old Church office building.

Gambling

During college and medical school I discovered I had an aptitude for cards and gambling. I didn't pursue it further until the mid 1970's when a high school friend looked me up. Jerry had become a regular Las Vegas gambler and I was intrigued by his stories. I made several trips to Las Vegas with him and I shared his rush for the excitement.

Although I was not a particularly high roller I had a quality that the casinos value as a player. That quality was my stamina and the amount of action that I showed. When I was in Las Vegas

I seldom slept. I was always at the tables gambling. The casinos know if they can get someone to spend enough time gambling, the player will eventually lose. The casino does not care if you win. They just want you to continue to play. I sweetened my appeal by establishing large lines of credit at most of the major casinos in Las Vegas and Lake Tahoe. This let the casinos know that when I broke down, their upside would be significant.

It turned into a mind game that I felt I could handle. It seemed less like gambling and more like adventure and intrigue. My plan was never to lose more than I would have been paying for the trip if I had not been "comped." I regularly won enough that my airfare, hotels, shows, and meals did not cost me a penny. This encouraged me to visit Las Vegas frequently.

For a while Yvonne went with me and a few times we took the family. There are family vacation opportunities available around Las Vegas if one wants to find them. Most visitors never realize there is a ski slope thirty minutes from downtown. The casinos don't discourage family vacations. They are like a patient spider, waiting for the fly to come back to the web.

Las Vegas is not a wholesome place and no matter how I try to sugar coat it; it didn't help my marriage. Things got worse when I became a card counter at Blackjack. I was able to keep track of the cards that have been played in a deck. When one can do this you can see times when the odds of winning turn in favor of the player. On those occasions you increase your bets significantly.

By adjusting your bets depending on the ratio of ten count cards remaining in the desk it is possible to statistically play so you will always win. The trouble is few people have the stamina or interest to play enough hands that these odds express themselves. Stamina was my forte.

Counting cards is not illegal but casinos don't like it. The next layer of thrill is trying to count cards without the casinos realizing it. When they are on to you they may kick you out of the casino. I was largely under their radar because I was making relatively small bets. I was winning regularly but not huge amounts of money. Still I was treated like a high roller because they were confident that if I spent enough time at the tables, I eventually would lose big. I saw it differently. I understood that the longer I played the more certain it was that I would win.

In those days there were no computers tracking the amounts and patterns that gamblers were betting. Neither could the casinos accurately know how much you are winning or losing. On one trip Yvonne and I were on the way to a medical meeting in Los Angeles with another couple and we stopped in Las Vegas. Of course our hotel, meals, and shows were complementary.

It was my custom to walk up to a blackjack table; they would recognize me and I would ask for and receive several thousand dollars in chips.

After a while I might leave that table, taking my chips on the table with me and proceed to another area of the casino. I would cash many of my chips at the cashier, being paid in one hundred dollar bills. When I returned to a different gambling table I would ask for more chips and sign a chit for them. If this went on through out the night I would end up with many hundred dollar bills. However, when checking out of the hotel I would write a check for my chits, giving the impression that I had lost several thousands of dollars.

My gambling era lasted about ten years. There was always the excitement of winning flavored with the intrigue of staying under the radar of the casino pit bosses. Las Vegas was a vacation for me. The excessive stimulation of the environment was revitalizing, as it is such a contrast from the way I lived my professional life in Dallas. I traveled to places I would not have been financially able to afford at the time. I liked playing the high rolling big shot.

This period in my life is nothing to brag about. Although it was never financially a disaster, I certainly never won enough money that it compensated for the financial and emotional impact of a divorce.

I no longer have lines of credit in the casinos. The few times I have gone back to Las Vegas, I am not comped and keep a low profile. I attend Church if I am there on a Sunday. The taxi drivers usually have to use their GPS to get me from the casinos to a Church.

Kathy says she finds Las Vegas depressing and distasteful. When we were dating I didn't realize she was so opposed to it. Similar to how when we were dating she got the impression that gardening was one of my favorite hobbies.

Thirty years being away from gambling, and thirty years of being married to Kathy have kept me safe. But is that the end of the story? Not long ago I was in St. Louis giving a medication lecture. On the way back to my hotel I noticed a tall, brightly lit, glass building. The driver told me it a Harrahs Casino. I asked him to stop there a few minutes, as I wanted to take a look. There was security at the casino entrance checking ID's. When the hostess checked mine, she asked me to wait. A few minutes later a distinguished older man dressed in a dark blue business suit walked toward me, stuck out his hand for me to shake, and said, "Welcome back Dr. Myers." It had been thirty years since I had been in a casino. The spider obviously had not given up.

Most casinos have stopped playing Blackjack with one deck, and now use a shoot that contains 8 decks. This makes card counting essentially impossible. This has also lessened my gambling temptation.

Not long ago I attended a neighborhood Texas Hold 'em tournament organized as a fundraiser for Katrina victims. To my surprise, I won the tournament. I had played poker pretty well during college and med school but was discouraged by the high importance of luck in winning. Texas Hold'em is betting against other players on the best poker hand, but five of the seven cards are mutually known and used. This makes it more possible to predict what two cards other players are holding and the strength of their hands. Like card counting in Blackjack, calculating odds is an essential factor in winning.

Texas Hold'em also requires reading people, not too dissimilar to psychiatry. The Katrina Tournament made me wonder if I might have some unique talent for playing Texas Hold'em. I have since won two of the last three tournaments I have entered. These were small entry fee, one hundred player tournaments. It is tempting to try a higher stakes game. That spider is probably getting excited.

More Real Estate Maneuvering

The house that Yvonne and I were living in was on an over-sized corner Beverly Dr. lot, a prestigious location in Highland Park. The house itself was a charming English tutor two story but needed updating.

My position was that we could make improvements over time and there was no way we could over-build the neighborhood. I felt it was a great investment.

Yvonne had liked where we were living on Caruth better, and was tired of moving. She had no interest in redoing and had her heart set that her next move would be into a new, modern residence. She had had her fill of my real estate deals; she had put up with enough. During my residency she had even lived for a while in a mental hospital.

When I bought the house on Beverly, I made a great real estate deal and gained a disgruntled wife. Yvonne never was happy in the Beverly house so when I thought I had an opportunity to rectify one of my marital errors, I took it.

One day Yvonne ran into a friend, Margaret. She and her husband, Bill, had just moved into a beautiful modern new home they had built on Dartmouth Ave, three blocks from our house on Beverly Dr. It was the kind of home Yvonne was dreaming about. Margaret, however, had become dissatisfied with the house during construction; Margaret preferred a house like ours that had more charm and a larger lot.

When I got home that evening I heard all about their meeting so I called Bill. He came over to our house and he loved it. We then went to his house and it looked good to me. Bill made a pitcher of martinis and we began to negotiate. Two hours later we had drawn up a contract. Two weeks later a moving van pulled up to Bill and Margaret's house, at the same time another arrived at ours, and by that evening we had switched houses.

We lived in Bill's modern new house for about 2 years. A new house came on the market on Dartmouth about three blocks east from where we were living. It was smaller and less luxurious, with no swimming pool. It was on a cul-de-sac that backed up to the Katy railroad track, less than one half a block from where I was building my office building. We sold our house, bought the new.

The deal generated enough cash that we were able to pay off all debt.

An interesting feature of the move from Dartmouth to three blocks down Dartmouth was my decision that it was too close to hire a moving van to move us. At the time I owned an unrestored 1959 Chevrolet pickup truck. I hired a hefty high school friend of our daughter to help me, and the two of us moved the complete household: furniture, appliances, piano and everything else, up and down stairs over a five day period. There was never a teenager who better earned his money. I haven't seen him since.

One debt paid off with this sale caused me particular satisfaction. When I made the decision to leave The University of Texas with two years of football eligibility still available, I had to forgo a fantasy that I would somehow make enough money to pay for a significant amount of the cost of my medical education. I was used to paying my way through college with a football scholarship. The compromise that Rosy and I worked out was he would loan me the money for medical school. He kept books on the note and interest, using it as an item in his financial statement when applying for loans for his construction company. My thought was it was like an insurance policy for him. I doubted that he would ever ask me to pay back the loan but if he needed the money, this would be a way of saving his pride. And that is the way it worked out.

Keeping books on the loan caused Yvonne and me to be more aware of the costs and sacrifice my parents were making. It caused us to make an effort to borrow less money. Yvonne worked as a bacteriologist at the medical school, I sold medical equipment to the other students, and we were managers of the apartment complex where we lived. My view is that loaning your children money for college is a model other families might emulate. I have written about it and mentioned it in talks. It was a very satisfactory arrangement for us.

Divorce and The Log Cabin

It was not long after we moved to the new house at the end of Dartmouth that Yvonne filed for divorce and we separated. At the time, this came as a big surprise to me. Now, looking back, I understand her position and am amazed that she was able to put up with me for twenty years. We spent two years seeing if we could salvage the marriage but there was just too much water under the bridge. The ending point came when she had a office party at our home (which she had the right to do) but which enraged me to a degree that I went over to the house and told everyone to leave.

That night, for the second time in my life I prayed. (The first was when we prayed for snow as a child.) My remorse and disappointment in myself manifested itself in an intense abdominal pain which felt as if someone was sticking a red hot poker into me. I prayed to God asking for relief. At "Amen" a sense of peaceful-ness came over me, the pain ceased, and I fell into a sound sleep. The next morning I was served with a restraining order and all rec-onciliation attempts ceased. One year later we were fairly amica-bly divorced.

Initially I moved into the apartment that Rosy and Jeri had occupied in the Old Church office building until a small rent house was found on Lovers Lane. There, for about six months, my friend Irv Ebaugh, recently separated, moved in with me. We made the best out of a bad situation and had some laughs over the similarity of our personalities to the actors in "The Odd Couple." As you might guess, I wasn't Felix.

During this period I sold the church office building so I needed to find a new office as well as a more permanent place to live. East of the Katy railroad train tracks, less than a block from the Dartmouth house where Yvonne was now living with little Dan and Belen, (Simone and Yvette were in college), was 20 acres of Dallas that essentially had become wilderness.

During the late 1800's – early 1900's it had been an area of small inexpensive houses where African-American families, most who worked as servants in Highland Park, lived.

Over the years the houses were abandoned, fell in ruin, and the forest took back the land. It was prime land for commercial development but title problems on the small residential lots whose owners had left no forwarding addresses made it unappealing to investors.

Rosy went to the courthouse and found an Illinois address for one lot's owner and Rosy gave him a call. Early in the conversation the owner warned Rosy that he would not sell the property for less than $15,000. By that afternoon I owned an office zoned lot with a clear title, sitting right on the boundary of Highland Park. Rosy and I began working on a design for a psychiatry office/apartment that would be appropriate for a wilderness setting. We decided on a log cabin that for thirty years was an icon for my private practice of child psychiatry. I lived in the log cabin for three years as a bachelor.

Log cabin office of Myers Psychiatry Clinic and apartment of Dr. Dan Myers

Yvette, Belen, Simone, and Little Dan had easy access to me at the log cabin. They could walk from Yvonne's house on Dartmouth across the Katy railroad track (1/2 block)

During that time I heard that a college friend who I had not seen in twenty years, Ann Mc Fadden Lawson, was dying of cancer. The cancer had spread to her bones and she was suffering badly. I was moved to call Ann, and to my surprise she said she had been thinking about calling me. Ann, a devout Christian, explained that she had been praying for her intractable pain to ease. However, she continued to suffer and wanted to know what psychiatry might offer for pain management.

Ann was unable to leave her bed so I met with her and her husband, Dr Ray Lawson at their home. We agreed that I would try hypnosis to relieve Ann's pain. Two to three times a week until her death eighteen months later, Ann and I worked together.

There appeared to be a marked lessening of her pain, and she was able to leave her bed and live a more normal life. It was always a disappointment, however, to find that her CAT scans showed no significant improvement and that her cancer continued to spread unabated.

During our sessions, Ann often discussed her feelings about having cancer, her impending death, the loss to her family, and the importance of her strong faith. I would listen with great empathy, struggling to find something to say that might be helpful to her.

Thirteen years after Ann's death, it began to dawn on me the role Ann had in directing me toward a more Christian life. When I wrote Ray to tell him of this revelation, he responded, "Dan, you never knew it, but from the very first she had been trying to save you." Thirty years after Ann's funeral while giving my first and only sermon in a church in Beijing, China I in mid-sentence was struck with the thought that Ann had kept her self alive, despite progressing painful cancer, in order to save me.

The Manic Alcoholic Olympics

While being separated and living at the log cabin it occurred to me that training for a marathon might be just the thing to more constructively fill my time and burn off my frustration and anger about our divorce proceedings.

It was a noble idea but it didn't turn out to be much of a character builder. Training with my buddies soon degenerated into a competition I ably named the "Manic Alcoholic Olympics." The log cabin was a perfect place for us to congregate. It was secluded, there were no neighbors, had a parking lot, a porch swing, a kitchen with a refrigerator for beer, a game room with a foosball table, a pool table, a side yard for pitching washers and a barbecue pit. The entire property and cabin was an ideal man cave.

Every Saturday Mike Trant, Jim King, and Craig Pairan would arrive at the log cabin at around 7:00 AM and we would start our run. The distance we would run depended on the stage of our training. It varied from a short 4 mile distance to running to White Rock Lake (5 miles), around the Lake (9miles) and back to the cabin (5 miles), total distance (19 miles). There were occasions when we would go around the lake twice before heading back to the cabin (total 27 miles). Then; Let the beer drinking begin!

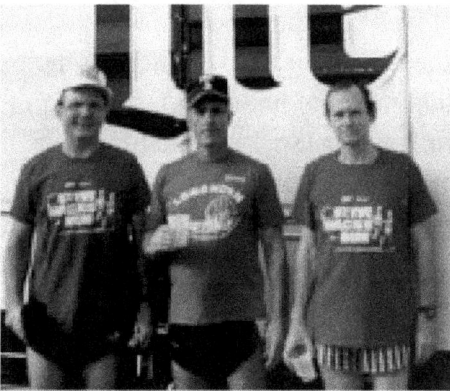

Dan   Mike Trant   Jim King   Craig Pairan

It would go on until midday, drinking, telling old sports stories and jokes, as we would go from one competition to another. First was washers, then darts, foosball, pool and on occasions rifle shooting set up inside the log cabin. During the year we competed in races of varying length.

Over a seven-year period I ran the White Rock, Boston, and New York Marathons, half marathons in Ft Worth, San Francisco, and Dallas, and numerous 10K runs. My best marathon time was at Boston, 3 hours and 14 minutes.

The first marathon I ran was the Dallas White Rock Marathon. I had heard that exercise, particularly running, could reduce stress, anger, and depression. Going through a divorce subjected me to all three. I bought Jim Fix's book, "How To Run A Marathon" and compulsively followed his schedule for preparation. Unfortunately I did not read all the chapters, the most significant one I missed being "Dangers and Risks."

The day of the marathon, the temperature was 84 degrees, unseasonably warm for December. Worse the humidity was close to 100%. Conditions were dangerous enough that because of heat related risk there was discussion of canceling the marathon.

Being inexperienced, I went out too fast so that when I hit the "wall" at about 22 miles, I was so exhausted that I considered quitting the race. However, there was a person calling out the pace of the runners and I learned that my pace had been fast enough that even if I walked the last 4.6 miles, I would cross the finish line in 3:30 hours, the cutoff time for 40 year olds to qualify for the Boston Marathon. At my level of exhaustion, walking is of no relief so I continue to jog at a slow plodding pace. The next thing I remember was falling thinking someone had run into me. I could not get up and was vomiting and short of breath. Two people were bending over me and I was able to get out the words, "I need help. I am a doctor. I believe I am having a heat stroke."

One of the two persons working on me somewhat impatiently said. "We both are doctors. I am on the faculty of the Dept. of Surgery at Southwestern Medical School; he is on the faculty of the Dept. of Medicine.

I was put into an ambulance and slowly moved through the crowd watching the race at the finish line. Although somewhat delirious I tried to tell the ambulance driver I wanted to be taken to Parkland hospital, known for treating the most serious emergencies. Fortunately, he paid no attention to me and I was taken to Doctor's Hospital, a hospital near White Rock Lake. They regularly treated racing problems and were equipped and experienced at treating heat stroke.

When the ambulance reached the ER I was immersed in a body-sized container of crushed ice. A young doctor was standing over me and asking me simple questions like my name, the date, and my address. I answered slowly and with difficulty. He asked me how long a marathon was and I could not remember. I remember thinking, 'I am going to be mentally disabled just because I ran this silly race."

As I was kicking myself for being so stupid, my attention was drawn to a bright light in the ceiling, seemingly encircled by fog. A sense of well being came over me and moments later I found myself floating up toward the ceiling and looking down on my body while a young intern was putting more ice on me. I remember being amused as he shook his hands, trying to lessen the cold from handling the ice. I do not know how long I was suspended in this state. A change in my sense of time was a major component of the characteristics of the phenomena. It was as if all worldly troubles were of no consequence. Leaving family didn't concern me as I had the thought that I would be seeing them again in the blink of an eye.

After a period of time, I found myself back in my body trying to answer questions from the intern. Several months after I recovered from the heatstroke, I researched the literature about out-of-body experiences. I discovered that my experience was similar to those reported by others.

In retrospect, it surprises me that I attached no religious significance to the experience. How more overtly could God show himself to me? He rescued me from death and enabled me to have more time on earth to be redeemed. Even though I had no religious beliefs or faith, the experience made it clear to me that there is afterlife. We will not dissolve back into the earth, going into some-

thing like a deep peaceful, nothingness sleep. Thank God He decide to not have me learn that from actually dying.

It convinced me we shall continue to exist. I also had the
thought that my experience was interrupted and incomplete and
that when I actually did die, I would learn more about what happens after you leave your body.

Although it sounds trite, it occurred to me that a deceased
is likely floating above his/her body for a few days and probably
observing the proceeding at visitation and at the funeral. (Interest-
ingly, it is the custom that the Jewish people bury their dead quickly. In the past there reasoning for this was that they believed the
soul tries to return to the body for three days and that quick burial
facilitates the soul/body separation).

No dramatic change occurred in my life immediately after
the heat stroke. I started to train for the Boston Marathon, determined that I would never again run a Marathon without better
training and preparation. The last two months before Boston I was
running 80 miles a week.

When not running with my buddies I would take a dog that
was being trained. Training hunting dogs, one dog at a time, had
become a hobby during my single days. Being single at the log
cabin was the perfect place. The dog in training was mostly isolat-
ed from other humans so there were very few distractions. Taking
a dog on a run would burn off a little of his excitement, and then he
was more attentive during the training session. Over the seven-
year period that I was single I trained a black Labrador Retriever,
an Irish Setter, and a Weimaraner

It was interesting to discover the traits and learning styles
of the different breeds. The Labrador was like a big happy oaf.
When running with him at heel I would carry a rolled up newspaper and whop him on his nose when he got out of line. He would
look back at me with a playful smile on his face. The Irish Setter
was much more sensitive. If discipline was too firm he became
cowed and would slink down and give me a hurt pitiful expression.
The only thing I found that was mild enough to keep up his self
esteem was a broom-straw. When he would surge too far forward I
would gently tap him on his snout and he would come back in line
without histrionics or despair.

When training was adjusted to fit their individual personalities each dog was an excellent student. Their tricks were mostly standard hunting dog routines but they were perfect at them. They would heal, sit, stay, go to their kennel, and retrieve directed by voice, hand or whistle commands. I taught the Weimaraner to wipe his feet before coming into the house. Everybody loved being with and interacting with these obedient well-behaved canines.

I sometimes explained that it was a cruel and selfish thing to allow a cute little puppy to grow into a large undisciplined teenage or young adult dog that would end up considered a nuisance and ignored in a back yard or kennel. The child rearing analogy was self-evident. There have been multiple occasions when I have had to bite my tongue to keep from telling a parent that my instructions for rearing their child came from what I had learned from dog training.

The log cabin had a wood-burning fireplace. I ordered a log splitting tool that was used like an ax. However, in place of a blade was a heavy triangular shaped wedge. It was amazing how when an upright log is struck with a wedge, it splits as effortlessly as if one was cutting through butter. Like Ronald Reagan, I found log splitting to be a surprisingly relaxing activity. If I had a patient cancellation or during a lunch break I often would go to the side yard and split logs.

One day at the top of a log splitting backswing a thought occurred to me. Why work so hard to make money in my practice if my greatest pleasure is having time to split logs? The 100 acres of land I owned from the Garden Valley Wilderness Camp was full of logs and only 20 miles from Tyler. I decided to try it out. I took a two-day a week consulting job at an MHMR clinic in Tyler helping them to develop a child psychiatry clinic. I began to think of living on my Garden Valley property, splitting logs, and working full time in Tyler. I bought and lived one night a week on a houseboat on Lake Palestine. Subsequently I bought a gingerbread style house in the historic area of Tyler that was known for its red brick streets. Rosy handled the purchase and remodeling.

It looked like the neighborhood around my Tyler house would soon convert to professional offices so a short time later I bought the three other adjacent lots. It fulfilled a childhood fantasy: I had a monopoly! I owned a city block. Unfortunately, I didn't hold them long enough for it to pay off like Boardwalk or Park Place.

Going through a divorce, driving back and forth to Tyler, and splitting logs limited the time I could spend being with the dog I was training, an Irish setter named George Washington. To find him a good home, I ran an add in the Dallas morning news. Two firemen who shared a house in the country came to check George out. I opened his kennel door and put him through his routine. The firemen were flabbergasted. One turned to the other and said, "Tom, there is a lot of traffic on Central Expressway today. What do you say, we let George drive home?"

TIME LINE

January 14, 1937 – Dan Allen Myers born in Paris, Texas
May, 1955 – Graduated Waco High School
September, 1955 – University of Texas
June, 1956 – Hacienda Santa Engracia, Mexico
July 1,1958 – Entered Baylor Medical School – Houston
June 5, 1959 – Married Yvonne Brown, Dallas
March 25, 1960 – Simone born
November 24 , 1961 – Yvette born
May 1962 – Graduated Baylor Medical School
July 1962 – Internship Methodist Hospital – Dallas
July 1963 – Captain US Army – San Antonio
November 24, 1964 – Belen born
July 1965 – Army discharge, began psychiatry residency
July 1969 - Finished adult & child psychiatry residency
May 11, 1972 – Little Dan Born
June 1977 Yvonne and I separated
1979 – Heat stroke at White Rock Marathon
April 1980 – Boston Marathon
June 1980 - Divorce Final -ended 21 year marriage
July 1980 - Moved into log cabin
July 1981 – Began dating Kathy
July 12, 1984 – Married Kathy Hawn and Lacy & Heather
     -Got full custody of little Dan
     -Gave up Tyler consulting job
     -Sold Garden Valley and Tyler property
     -Reopened Myers Psychiatry Clinic in the log cabin
     -Joined Highland Park Presbyterian Church
     -Gave up credit lines in Las Vegas.
     -Stopped drinking for 10 years
     -Stopped splitting logs
     -Resigned - Manic Alcoholic Olympics

Remarrying

Saying "A marriage is made in Heaven" probably applies to most of us as we look back and wonder about the unique circumstances that resulted in us getting to the alter. The 9 year difference in our age alone would have made it unlikely that we would meet. Kathy grew up in Houston in a devout Lutheran family where the Bible and the Church was their guiding force. Her parents lived conservatively with little fanfare and no debt. When Kathy left for college she moved from the home her parents had purchased when they married and where they continued to live until her father's death.

I was reared in Waco where my father, a contractor, lived his life vacillating from almost rich to having the bankers ready to foreclose on one of the multiple homes we lived while growing up. Kathy's dad's mantra was "live within your means." My father kept us on a financial rollercoaster, living in the fast lane on borrowed money. The Lutheran Church shaped Kathy's values; mine by Ridgewood Country Club in Waco. Psychological prenuptial testing showed Kathy and I set the record for the greatest personality differences between potential spouses. Impulsive, risk-taking, dominated my scale and Kathy just as high on the conservative, cautious side. How could it happen that we would marry in 1984?

Think about this coincidence (?): In August 1968 during the final year of my child psychiatry residency, my Army friend Dr. Jack Harrison had just started an OB/GYN practice in Texarkana Arkansas. He and his wife invited my first wife, Yvonne, and me to Texarkana for the weekend. The Harrisons gave a party beginning early Saturday afternoon to introduce us to their friends. It was 102 degrees outside when one of the women at the party announced that her 10-year-old son had locked himself in the car and refused to get out. She was legitimately panicked by the thought that the intense heat might kill him. The guests in attendance began to discuss how to get him out of the car. At that point Jack made an announcement to the group, "Have no fear, our guest, Dr. Dan Myers, Dallas Child Psychiatrist will handle this situation" and he showed me to the door.

The heat from the outside was stifling. Walking toward the car the crowd inside the house gathered at the windows to observe. Finishing the last of my beer I looked inside the car. Staring back at me was a sweaty, tough looking, defiant bur headed boy. Tapping on the window with the beer can the boy watched attentively as I slowly crushed the can flat and said, "See what I did to that can? That's what I am going to do your head if you don't open that door." The door swung open and putting my hand gently on the boy's shoulder we walked back into the house. The guests were awed and applauded as we entered.

Fast forward from 1968 sixteen years to January 1984. For seven years I had been single. Kathy and I had been dating for the last three. Her conservative Lutheran family was becoming worried that she might be getting serious about a psychiatrist. Kathy's sister, Marcille, at a Houston luncheon, mentioned that her younger sister was dating a Dallas psychiatrist.. One of the ladies asked his name and Marcille told them. To this, the women exclaimed, "Dr Dan Myers? I know who he is. He was at a party in Texarkana in 1968 and I saw him gently talk a little boy out of a dangerously overheated locked car. He saved the boy's life. He is wonderful!

Who would have ever thought that incident would someday be pivotal in my being accepted by a future unknown wife. Someone upstairs must have known I was going to need all the help available.

When one is making a very big decision it helps to have confirming signs from Heaven. My divorce left me with a well-used family station wagon. I rented a car and listed the station wagon for sale in the want adds. When the ad came out, it was next to an ad from a person wanting to trade silver flatware for a station wagon. By that afternoon the station wagon had been replaced by a bag of silver knives, forks and spoons. The bag was placed under my bed and wasn't given another thought until shortly before Kathy and I married. When Kathy opened the bag she excitedly exclaimed, "Old Master! My pattern!" Another good sign?

The first time Kathy's parents met me was not an impressive début. Martin and Lucile Nerger came to Dallas in December to celebrate Kathy's December 9th birthday. I made a reservation for dinner at Benihana's not appreciating the significance that it was on December 7.

When Kathy told her father where we were going he fumed saying, "What type of American would celebrate in a Japanese restaurant on Pear Harbor day?" Kathy and her mother, Lucile, eventually convinced Martin to go but during the evening Lucile could not be drawn into conversation. She later told Kathy that she "wasn't about to have any psychiatrist analyze her."

Nevertheless, time seemed to satisfy most parental reservations about our marriage. Lucille couldn't have been a better mother-in-law. Having one whose fear of being analyzed causes her to be a little less out spoken isn't all bad. Kathy grew up a strong Daddy's girl and most of the family agreed Martin and I had a lot in common. We got along well and since his death in 1990 I really miss him. He was a tough, hard headed German-American but very interesting and fun to be around.

The following story is a good example of his personality and humor. Kathy's parents were visiting us at our newly remodeled home. They had come to help us with some of the unfinished improvements. Kathy, Lucile, Martin and I were finishing breakfast when I asked him how his estrogen treatment for his recently diagnosed prostate cancer was going. He glanced across the table to make sure Kathy and Lucile were listening and answered, "OK but every since I have been taking female hormones all I want to do is sit on my ass."

Martin's memory continues to provide me a little slack. Whenever Kathy gets really fed up with me, I put on Martin's cowboy hat he willed me and everything is OK.

Kathy and I were married at Highland Park Presbyterian Church the afternoon of Saturday July 12, 1984. Only our children were present for the ceremony.

Simone Myers Howell, David Howell, Belen Myers, Dan Sr, Yvette Myers
Bottom row: Heather Hawn, Dan Jr, Kathy Hawn Myers, Lacy Hawn

You may have noticed that the groom in the wedding pictures above has more hair than you remember. Permanently getting rid of my toupee was largely motivated by an event that occurred shortly after Kathy and I were married. I was in the kitchen as Kathy was preparing dinner for Marcille and Bonham Magness (her sister and brother in law) and friends Dr. Moody Alexander and his wife, Freddie. Kathy baked a package of frozen dinner rolls and when they had finished she sprinkled fresh flour on them giving them an appearance of being homemade. I, mostly kidding, told Kathy that this was "cheating." She let it pass and we discussed it no further.

However, during the dinner, Freddie commented on the wonderful rolls and she asked Kathy for her recipe. Kathy, looked at Freddie, then to me, and said, "Dan, why don't you tell them about the rolls."

I don't remember, but surely I must have had several glasses of wine, because I began by explaining in a carefully worded and drawn out statement how in my family we had a very strong ethic about not lying and that in Kathy's family there evidently was more leeway about white lying and other forms of mild untruthfulness. Then I told them about the flour sprinkling. There was a long silence. Then her sister, Marcille, asked, "Dan, You don't consider wearing a toupee a white lie?"

We spent the first night of our marriage at the log cabin with Kathy's two girls and Little Dan.

Little Dan   Lacy   Heather

The next morning we put all three children on the bus to Camp Longhorn. On Sunday, Kathy and I checked into the Mansion hotel. I had ordered the Honeymoon package with considerable difficulty as the clerk continually assumed I meant the "Anniversary package." Despite my concern that there would be Happy Anniversary signs in our suite, it turned out he got it right.

The honeymoon suite was opulent and large. We ordered up alcohol and hors d'oeuvres, called some friends and before we knew it we had a real wedding reception.

While the children were at camp, we moved into a rental property near the house we were remodeling. The house we bought was directly across the alley from the home where Kathy and her girls had been living. This was important to Kathy as she had read that a move for teenager's is psychologically traumatic. Yvonne agreed to give us custody of Dan Jr. and thus we began our marriage as a blended family.

Our first important family project was to clean the construction site of our future home each weekend. This was done with some initial grumbling but over time fostered family bonding, pride, and anticipation of an upcoming move.

Lacy   Dan Jr.   Kathy   Heather Dan Sr.

The day of our move happened to fall on the Children's Medical Center's fundraiser held at Six Flags Over Texas. The children, Kathy, and I, received some criticism from other parents who felt my insistence the children help with the move, rather than go to Six Flags was "cruel and unusual punishment."

Becoming a Church Guy

Kathy, Heather and Lacy were members at Highland Park Presbyterian Church so Little Dan and I started attending with them. During a sermon one morning, the thought came to me that I had never read a biography of Jesus Christ. I picked up a Bible and began reading in the New Testament. I was amazed at the explicit descriptions of Jesus and his culture. I read the New Testament with equal interest as I previously had read great historical fiction. About that same time, Kathy convinced me to attend a Bible Study.

In the Bible Study there were occasions when I questioned the Bible's validity. It was embarrassing to hear from the more informed members that the answer would be found in parts of the Bible I had yet to read. I resolved to read the entire Bible within the upcoming year.

Hoping to learn how some Muslims could justify their barbaric violence, I had already begun reading the Koran. The Koran is written as poetry, with no clear storyline, and for me it was so boring that after 50 pages I was ready to abandon it. There were 365 more pages to read in the English translation I was using.

A thought occurred! Following the schedule for "Walk Through The Bible" would require 365 days. Reading one page of the Koran after each Bible assignment should be bearable. One year later I had finished both the Bible and the Koran. I found nothing in the Koran justifying the nature and the degree of the perpetrations reported in the news. If Muslims would test their own faith by reading and comparing it against the Bible, they should see how far off track they have become. Unfortunately if they are discovered reading literature about other religions they may be subject to persecution or death.

Reading the Koran, contrary to the stated concern of some of my Christian friends, reinforced my journey to Christian belief. It satisfied the argument that I should not judge the Koran when I had never read it. We make considerable effort to see that Muslims in the US have free speech and other liberties that Americans enjoy. Christians are not allowed to visit Mecca. If we make a statement that is less than pious about Mohammed, we risk being beheaded. Our government pushes for integration of Muslims into our culture. Islam publicly states that their mission is to destroy American "Crusaders." The horrors of the Crusades apply to both peoples. However, with the help of Jesus Christ, and time, we grew out of it.

The mini-tirade above is chronologically out of context. At the time Kathy and I were blending our two families, the Muslims were not our primary interest. More important were issues like assuring that twelve year olds Lacy's and Little Dan's fraternal relationship did not turn romantic, and dealing with fifteen year old Heather's position that, "You are not my real father and you can't tell me what to do." My answer to Heather was always the same, "Heather, you are one half right."

Soon we moved into our newly remodeled house where thirty-one years later we still live. Kathy and I returned to our routines; me working in child psychiatry, Kathy in real estate, and the children in school.

In 1984 when Kathy and I married I would have said I was a Christian. However, I had never read the Bible, seldom went to Church, nor lived by Christian principles. Married to Kathy, Dan Jr. and I began to attend Highland Park Presbyterian Church on Sundays. Kathy got a mutual friend, Dr. Moody Alexander to invite me to attend a Bible Study with him. Thirty-one years later I continue to attend.

One distinction between me and the other members were our Bibles. Theirs' were battered and frayed, smudged and marked by underlining and their handwritten notes in the margins. Mine was new and clean from lack of use. It made me feel much like sitting on the bench in a football game while the team is struggling with another team in mud and rain. When the coach sends you onto the field to replace an injured player you stand out like Casper the Ghost in your sparking pristine unsoiled uniform.

This issue was solved one morning when I placed my Bible on the top of my car while balancing a cup of coffee. Running a little late in bad weather the Bible was forgotten. Arriving at Church, the Bible of course was gone. I drove back home, retracing my route. Sure enough it was crumpled near a curb. It had been run over. Its stained and rumpled pages made me feel much more comfortable and less obviously a rookie in the group.

The more I read the Bible the more enthralled I became. In retrospect I recognize that some force outside myself, the Holy Spirit, was changing my interests and attitude. My interest in secular literature, even historical fiction, lessened. Over the next twenty years I continued to be drawn to religious literature. I began to write and teach comparing psychiatry and modern child rearing principles to the principles found in the Bible.

Over time I became convinced the Bible was God's word and I studied diligently to see if God had a plan for me. Having not been a religious leader in my first family, I was eager to share what I was now learning with my adult children. This effort resulted in a book, published by the Paulist Press, entitled Golden Rules for Parenting, A Child Psychiatrist Discovers the Bible. Soon I was invited to teach and lecture at various Church groups. I was becoming known as a "Church guy."

First Mission Trip - Cuba

While preparing for service as a Deacon at Highland Park Presbyterian Church I was assigned to teach a lesson on self indulgence. Throughout the Bible there are references to self indulgence being a sin. This, for me, was hard to accept because it seemed normal to want to improve one's life circumstances. Who doesn't want to eat in a better restaurant, stay at a higher quality hotel, fly first class rather than coach, fly in a private plane rather than commercial, etc. I had that read the Pope came to the US in a private jet that had been adapted to provide sleeping quarters and a dining room with a kitchen to prepare foods for his special tastes.

One night at a wedding reception I happened to be sitting next to Woody Strodel, a Presbyterian minister. I mentioned how difficult it seems to avoid the sin of self indulgence. He responded immediately with a question, "Have you ever been on a mission trip?"

The next morning in our Bible study it was announced a mission trip to Cuba had a member cancel. I immediately signed up. It was not that I felt I was being directed by the Holy Spirit or that it was God's will for me to go. I took it as a coincidence that a minister had mentioned it the night before. For years I had wanted to try Cuban cigars and I was curious about Cuba as it was off limits for American tourists.

The trip was sponsored through East/West Ministries. I attended an orientation session, assuming my service would be in some medical capacity. Instead, the mission was primarily evangelical. Religious tracts were passed out giving suggestions on how to approach Cubans about Jesus.

The trip was planned for March 1999, a time when the Cuban embargo was still enforced. The US government permitted Church visits to Cuba under a humanitarian exemption. Cuba, however, seldom approved Americans humanitarian visas.

Our mission group left Dallas flying first to Cancun, Mexico. From Cancun we transferred to a Cuban airline to Havana saying we were tourists rather than a church ministry.

An important goal of our trip was to transport Bibles through Cuban customs. I asked how we would do this since Cuba is a Communist atheist country and it is illegal to take Bibles into Cuba. The leader's response wasn't that reassuring to me, as he handed me eight Bibles to hide in my luggage. He said, "We will pray them in." To my astonishment, even though the Havana airport was well staffed with military personnel carrying machine guns, all the Bibles passed through customs without a hitch.

Getting through customs unscathed was a relief, but did little to lessen my considerable anxiety about being in a communist country illegally. The best practical advice about staying safe came from my son who was working in Edmonton, Canada. He said, "Dad, remember these words,'Don't shoot! I am a Canadian."

Although I was the oldest person on the trip, I had been a Christian for the shortest period of time. Most of the group had been on several short mission trips and some had been missionaries. This was my first mission trip and I had little knowledge about how we would proceed or what was expected from me. My abrupt decision to make the trip did not allow time to study and review information about the history, culture, or religious beliefs of the people to whom we would soon be evangelizing.

The twenty member Cuban mission team included four East-West staff and sixteen volunteers coming from Highland Park Presbyterian or Bent Tree Bible Fellowship Churches. We spent the first night in Havana at the Hotel de Sevilla which was once a grand hotel. Like most of the places we visited; it was in poor repair and short on service (pretty typical third world communist run country.)

The morning of our first day in Cuba was orientation. It was explained that as representatives of a Christian Church no alcohol or cigar smoking was permitted So much for one of my underlying motives for the trip.

The orientation continued with a review of the various techniques and approaches we might use to guide others to accept Christ. We were each assigned a Cuban interpreter who would accompany us as we went door to door through a village. We left Havana Saturday afternoon on a chartered modern bus. Our East-West staff had selected several small rural villages outside of Havana where we were told most people had never heard the Gospel.

On the bus I tried to prepare and brace myself for a very uncomfortable experience. How was I going to convince a person I had never met from a culture I didn't know, in a foreign language to commit to a religion which I had just begun to accept. I could think of only one strength that might permit me to perform adequately. This was my ability to speak Spanish. Unfortunately forty years had passed since I worked in Mexico and was fluent. My interpreter, Raymon, helped me in writing my script in Spanish. By the time we knocked on our first door I had it memorized.

I was terrible!! Thank God, Ramon, a strong Christian, would step in when I was floundered. I had never felt so inadequate and out of my element. If there was any way I could have gotten back to Dallas I would have skedaddled. When our group returned that evening to the hotel there was excitement and enthusiasm. Members were shouting congratulations to one another as they described how they had brought five, or more people to Christ that afternoon. More than a hundred people had been lead to

Christ that day. I didn't do my part. I might qualify for one or two "assists" but I could not in clear conscious say that I had brought anyone to Jesus.

That evening in bed I prayed, telling God I couldn't do it and that if there was anyway possible, please let me off this hook. As I prayed I felt a wave of comfort come over me and I drifted off into a sound sleep.

The next morning I tore up my Spanish translation script and told Raymon I would do the sessions in English with him translating. Our first stop was in a humble home that had a large extra room with several tables and chairs. The couple who lived in the home had a small business operating a restaurant. I began my presentation with the idea that I would convey my feelings about so late in life becoming a Christian, trusting that Raymon would convey my words in a way that might be meaningful.

The couple was very attentive and began to ask me questions that Raymon would translate. As the time passed other people seeing us in the room though the open door as they walked by, came into the room and took seats at the tables. Soon there were 20 or so villagers listening to our discussion. As the questions came I found that I understood them perfectly and to most of them I automatically began to respond in clearly understood Spanish. By the time we finished, fifteen people stepped forward and signed cards saying they accepted Jesus Christ as their Lord and savior.

As the day progressed and we knocked on the doors of other homes the success rate of my evangelism effort continued to expand. When we returned to the hotel that evening I was as excited and exhilarated as the others. When the card count was tabulated that day I led the class.

As I look back on that day sixteen years ago (reading my journal from the trip) I marvel at the improvement that day in my ability to speak and understand Spanish. There is a place in the Bible, *Acts 2: 5-8,* where the Holy Spirit helped a foreign language to be understood. What I needed was just a little bit of rustiness to be removed which should be no big task for the Holy Spirit. Keep in mind, these thoughts are in retrospect. When I was on the mission trip I hadn't read Luke's account of Pentecost. My thoughts at the time were more on the order of, "Great job, Dan."

Back at the hotel the next morning, reality slammed in. Two armed Cuban soldiers confronted our group and ordered us to get back on our bus and follow their vehicle to the immigration office, as we were under arrest for being in Cuba illegally and for preaching and imposing a religion on citizens of the Communist atheist state of Cuba. My revelry from the night before quickly disappeared, and my anxiety from the previous days accelerated.

Others in our group continued to maintain an angelic happiness and good humor seeing this only as a slight bump in the road and an opportunity to demonstrate their faith. Next to fear, my second most prevalent thought was that I didn't have much in common with the other members of our group.

As we loaded onto the bus one of our group took a picture of the guard and there was an ugly confrontation as he demanded to know who had taken a picture and he wanted the camera confiscated. No one would tell who took the picture and he became increasingly enraged. We finally got on the bus with an armed guard accompanying.

As we made our way to the immigration compound the group commenced to sing hymns. Along the way one of the women in our group suggested that we lay hands on one of the members who had come down with a sore throat. She began to pray over the ill member commanding loudly that Satan come out of his body and that Satan cease his attack on our mission as we were under the protection of Jesus Christ. The closest I came to reverence was murmuring under my breath, "Heaven help me, what am I doing here"

The immigration building was what you might imagine from a movie set. We were herded into a large tile atrium and told to sit on the floor. There was a balcony surrounding the atrium with armed soldiers on it looking down on us. Two officers came forward and called the name of Maria, a member of the Bent Tree group who had escaped Cuba as a child. She was taken away by the officers and we stayed seated on the floor until she was brought back in tears approximately two hours later.

She explained to us that the Cubans knew that we had come into Cuba pretending to be tourists when we actually were missionaries and that they had prepared documents for us to sign acknowledging our guilt. Our written confession was passed around for us to read and sign. I was able to read the Spanish document and what they accused us of was true. However one of our members stood up and announced that we could not sign the document because it was written in a foreign language and we were unable to understand the charges against us. The officers left in frustration.

About thirty minutes later one of them returned. Then we heard about two hours of "good cop-bad cop" routine. The good cop, Lieutenant Guerra explained that he understood our visit was well intended and that if it was only up to him he was inclined to look the other way and release us. However, Captain Perez, the "bad cop" became increasingly frustrated by the group's lack of cooperation and disrespectful attitude. If it were entirely up to Captain Perez he would put us under arrest until the matter could be handled through negotiations with the U S State Department. Captain Perez's opinion was that we were as equally in violation of the US embargo as we were of Cuban law.

Finally we were released with the strict admonition that we were in Cuba on a tourist visa and we had better behave like it. There would be no more evangelizing, we would attend no more Cuban house churches, distribute no more Bibles nor hymnals, and we would conduct ourselves in a manner that did not draw attention to our being a religious group.

We were released and returned to our bus. Immediately, a conference began about whether we should abide by their commands or defy them. The general attitude was that we, like the Apostle Paul, should continue to preach the Gospel and to evangelize even with the risk of imprisonment. Acts 20:22-24 says ,"And now, compelled by the Spirit, I am going to Jerusalem, not knowing what will happen to me there. I only know that in every city the Holy Spirit warns me that prison and hardships are facing me. However, I consider my life worth nothing to me; my only aim is to finish the race and complete the task the Lord Jesus has given me—the task of testifying to the good news of God's grace."

During the previous four days of the Cuba trip I had kept as low a profile as I could manage. I never contributed to the discussion or decision making nor did anyone ask for my opinion. I was the lowest person of influence as I was a new Christian and had come on the mission trip on an impulse, thinking I would be contributing as a physician. However this was getting so serious I spoke up, "I can remember very little scripture but a passage comes to mind from somewhere in the Bible, 'Well done good and faithful servant." I went on to say that over a hundred people had already been brought to Christ and my view was we had done a good job. My recommendation was that we finish our Cuban mission as tourists and go home.

My opinion was given weight commensurate with my time as a Christian and my previous missionary experience. They decided we would take one day off and go to a beach and act like other tourists. We knew this would be reported to authorities because we had good evidence that our bus driver was an informant. The group would abandon the original plan of working with two specific churches as this would easily be recognized as defiance.

After our day on the beach, we would use hit and run tactics driving over Cuba looking for individuals who were earnestly seeking God. By not staying in one location for any significant period of time we hoped to stay ahead of the government's tracking, yet still find people to convert.

The result was 23 additional people accepted Christ. Of the last 23 I had one. I was alone jogging on a beach at a hotel outside of Trinidad the night before we were returning to Havana. As I ran I said a prayer thanking God that we were not in prison and also declaring to Him that I considered myself off evangelist duty. Just as the words were out of my mouth, a young Cuban man named Edwardo stepped out of the brush and onto to the beach and began to run beside me. He began to ask me questions about my faith. He ran with me to the hotel where he signed a card accepting Christ. I gave him some Woolite and the remainder of my dirty clothes. He left saved and ecstatic.

After a tourist-like visit of Trinidad on Saturday March 13 we drove back to the Hotel Sevilla in Havana. At 9:30 that night our leaders said we were off of missionary duty and free to smoke a cigar and have a drink. Several of us, including two of the ministers, walked over to the restaurant, La Bodequita, a favorite place of Hemingway. We ordered pork, beans and rice and mojitos topped off with a Cohiba Cuban cigar. This is what I had thought Cuba would be like.

When I got back to the hotel I tried my first call back to the states. I wanted to tell Kathy we were trying to catch an earlier flight out of Cancun the next morning. It was difficult making the Havana/ Dallas connection and when I finally got through Kathy almost hung up on me. Because we had the suspicion that our phone might be tapped and our room bugged I was speaking very softly. She didn't recognize my voice, and initially thought I was an obscene phone caller.

Reflections on Cuba Trip:

Secular: From a secular perspective the trip was informative. I fulfilled a long time wish to visit Cuba, a country that was forbidden to most Americans. I found the people of Cuba to be welcoming of Americans despite the unresolved conflict between the two countries.

Cuba is third-world-like. Nothing is new or well maintained since the Russians left the island in 1964. When we were there in 1999 the whole country appeared in disrepair. Visiting Cuba reinforced my views of the great danger the United States faces as it drifts more toward socialism.

The Cuban people are poor. The usual salary for a sales clerk was $7.00 a day. A medical doctor made $12/day. They must shop for their groceries in government stores that will take pesos. The people were paid in pesos and can be sent to prison if they attempt to use dollars. There are limited goods available. Often it is necessary for the poor to turn to the black market. Black market prices are greatly inflated and there is always the danger of being arrested. The electricity is turned off by the government during certain times of the day. Stray dogs and cats are pitifully thin. Cattle are malnourished. Even the plants and landscapes are dry and neglected.

Typical appearance of a Cuban car in March 1999

There are few cars. Most are models that were purchased prior to the Russian exit in 1964. Cubans keep the old cars running by patching them with parts scavenged from other old cars or with whatever else they can find. There are no new factory replacement parts available.

There are two areas that the Cuban Government points to with pride. One is the education provided for the people that is said to have produced a literacy rate near100%. The other is the availability and quality of their medical care. They claim all Cubans have access to medical care and that doctors trained in Cuba are recruited to serve in other Latin Countries. From what I saw during my short stay in Cuba, medical care was not impressive. Although minor illnesses and complaints may be quickly and satisfactorily addressed, there were long waiting lists for surgery. The quality of the system was extremely compromised by the lack of modern equipment and medicines. For example one of our group was bringing a supply of disposable needles for a diabetic Cuban patient who had been reusing dull and questionably sterile needles.

In 1999 what was even more painful to see was their loss of personal liberty. There was a strong military presence throughout Cuba. It is common to see soldiers armed with automatic weapons. Cubans are not allowed to travel out of the country. They are not allowed to rent cars. Hotels can not register Cuban citizens. No hunting is allowed in Cuba and no private ownership of guns is permitted. Since Cuba is Communist, it is an atheist state and practicing a religion is against the law. My impression was that the government does not rigidly enforce this restriction but depending on the varying political climate, churches are subjected to being closed and the members being arrested. Every block has a communist leader who monitors and reports illegal or suspicious activity. Cubans who will be having contact with Americans must clear it with the block leader. Being too involved with US citizens can cause a Cuban to lose a job, government benefits. or receive jail time.

I feel fortunate that I was able to see aside of Cuba that most tourists would never see. It turned out that having to cancel our planned agenda and driving through Cuba in a random fashion was a blessing ; we were able to see more Cuba territory. Being arrested and threatened wasn't pleasant but it sure was unique and gave me more to talk and write about. The beaches and water at Trinidad and Cayo Coco were pristine and I anticipate the fishing will be wonderful if Cuba finally opens up.

I couldn't smoke Cuban cigars during the trip but the U.S. embargo allowed citizens to spend $100 on goods while in Cuba. Using your quota for cigars was permitted. I brought $100 worth back to Dallas. From a secular point of view, the trip was informative, adventurous, and safe. I felt fortunate to have had the experience,

Theological:

It is difficult and embarrassing for me to tease out the various ways this trip impacted my faith. Not growing up in a family where religion was emphasized and since having most of my adult life surrounded myself with people who also never gave theology any thought, evangelizing in Cuba with our mission group was a shock.

I had never been in close contact with a group of people who were so religious. These people seemed very different from me. They marched in a light I had never seen. Even more unsettling was becoming aware that their views may be more the norm than mine.

When I had the out-of-body experience nearly 20 years previous, the most significant take away message for me was that there is life after death. It seems strange this revelation did not shock me into learning more about this phenomena. Nor did it seem to make me more religious. I had little interest in the supernatural. If science didn't endorse it, neither would I.

To these people on the Cuba trip the supernatural was of primary importance. This life on earth seemed to have lesser significance to them than the new life they would experience after death. This was probably the reason they showed less concern than I did about being arrested.

During the early years my marriage to Kathy I noticed that she and her daughters seemed to have peace of mind and comfort, but until the Cuba trip it never occurred to me this had anything to do with religion. The Cuban mission opened my eyes.

Becoming aware there are many people in this world living with a different concept of reality than I have was a shock. It was a jump start to opening my mind and exploring more of the concept of faith. The Cuba experience was an important stimulus for my study of the Christian Bible and the theology of other world religions.

The Cubans to whom we ministered, despite being poor, subject to persecution, and having limited opportunity for improvement under the Communist government, were happy, grateful and generous. They joyfully shared the little that they had with others.

Although my exposure to Christians in the US has been limited, I had noticed that most of the men in my Frank Hundley Mens Discussion Bible Study have a remarkably calm, warm, even-tempered, kind, demeanor. These and similar positive attributes have been named by the Apostle Paul as the Fruit of the Spirit.

Galatians **5:22** "But the fruit of the Spirit is love, joy, peace, forbearance, kindness, goodness, faithfulness, gentleness and self-control."

Christian Cubans manifest these fruit. Going to Cuba underscored my desire to develop them. It increased my resolve to continue my study of Christianity and my association with the men in the weekly Frank Hundley Bible Study.

In Cuba the power of prayer was more evident. The Cuban people, desperate and broken by Communism, rely on their faith to protect and empower them. They pray frequently, and confidently to Jesus. Many of the house churches we visited had members who testified how they had been healed by God.

Not having grown up in a Christian atmosphere and having in adult life been emerged in a highly secular educational and scientific environment, I had developed a mildly disdainful attitude toward religion and its leaders. Until Cuba I had had little personal contact with ministers. Those leading our Cuban mission were as talented, industrious and intelligent as any people I had met. Two of our Cuban group, Jay Lee and Howard Griffin, already successful young business men, subsequently left their worldly vocations, went to seminary and are now outstanding ministers.

The failure of my scholarly attempt to deliver my testimony in carefully prepared Spanish and the success that resulted when I abandoned my own efforts and asked for God's help was a revelation to me. However, striving for self reliance and being prideful continues to be problematic. Seeing how easily and comfortable the members of our group and the Cuban Christians were with explaining and defending their faith convinced me the source of their wisdom was the Bible. My knowledge was deficient and I resolved to become better informed.

After going on a mission trip to Cuba, being arrested, and experiencing religious insights, I kept waiting for the next shoe to drop. Nothing dramatic has been recognized.

The Frank Hundley Bible Study has been uniquely beneficial for me. It bridged a gap for me as I transitioned from worldly friends to those with Christ-centered values. Our Bible study has been a great place for clarification and explanation of Scripture. When I read passages that make no sense to me or seem contradictory, other members provide fresh insights. The group holds each of us accountable to stay on a Christian path and provides men with strong character to emulate. A good fit in a Bible Study group is a great blessing for any Christian.

I became an enthusiastic Bible student. Bible reading showed me there were child-rearing directions in the Bible that were similar to what I tried to teach the parents of my child psychiatry patients. I began to write down my comparison of Biblical child rearing direction with modern psychiatric teaching about parenting. The result was a book, <u>Golden Rules For Parenting, A Child Psychiatrist Discovers the Bible,</u> published by the Paulist Press. The first year it was a best seller at Logos, a popular Dallas religious bookstore but subsequently sales dwindled. In 2008 I was notified by Paulist Press that it would not be reprinted.

It seemed God wasn't interested in my giving up child psychiatry and becoming a Christian author, but there were signs that I was changing: I became a regular attendee at Church and Bible Study, a frequent guest lecturer in Sunday Schools and I cheerfully began to tithe. My language and jokes became cleaner; I was asked to say the blessing at meals and my alcohol consumption decreased.

Second Mission Trip - Romania

One of my Christian friends in the Frank Hundley Bible Study is Jim Vandemeer. Jim has a daughter, Catherine, who married a missionary, Bruce Thomas, and they were living in Romania. Jim would periodically talk about Catherine and their ministry in the Bible Study. Six years after returning from Cuba for unknown reason I began to have a strong urge to visit Romania. No planned church group was found going to Romania. Kathy was unable to go with me and I was reluctant about going by myself. I decided to ask my cousin Bob.

Bob Crosby, two years younger than I, grew up in Shreveport, Louisiana. During childhood he sometimes would spend summers in Waco with our family. After childhood we lost track of each other, but after my divorce he got back in touch. We became and still are are close friends.

Bob, grew up of humble means but he became a successful, self-made entrepreneur. His work activity involved considerable travel and his primary recreation is boating. Bob's wife, Judy, now deceased, had an aversion to travel and he began to invite me on some of his jaunts, particularly on boat trips when he needed more crew.

Although Bob says he is a Christian he has a a pretty egocentric view of what this entails. A secondary motive for inviting Bob to go with me to Romania was that I hoped to further evangelize him.

Bob wasn't enthusiastic about Bruce's ministry in Romania but he was very interested in beginning our trip with touring Prague and Budapest. He said he would plan the first five days of our trip and I could plan the last five days in Romania.

So on January 30, 2006 Bob flew into Dallas and we finalized our preparations. Europe was having an unusually cold winter. The temperatures in Prague and Budapest were below zero Fahrenheit. Neither of us knew about weather that cold. Bob was a world traveler but much of it had been working with Hospital Corporation of America in Saudi Arabia.

We made a trip to a ski store to purchase "Hot Chili's" long underwear and a heavy parka for Bob. The coups de grace of my zero degree packing was my son-in-law, Andrew's fur Cossack style hat he had bought when in Moscow 10 years earlier.

Kathy took us to DFW Airport February 1st. I had a Bible in a carryon planning to start my Bob-conversion shortly after takeoff. However, Bob had set us up in Business Class travel and most of the flight was consumed with being served luscious meals and drinks Our transfer to British Airways at Gatwick for the flight to Prague went similarly - no Bible talk.

Prague was beautiful in the snow. Bob and I took a walk around the hotel but didn't venture far because of the cold and also because we hadn't had much sleep. The next morning a driver Bob had arranged picked us up in his big Mercedes. Accompanying the driver was our guide, Radka Voctkova, a blond who looked straight out of a James Bond movie.

Bob Crosby in Prague
with Radka Voctkova

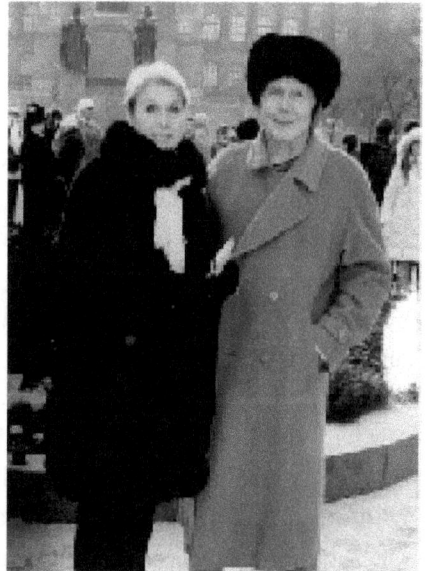

Radka with Dan
Wearing Andrew's hat.

The rest of the day Bob and I stumbled over each other trying to impress her. It was a competition I had no possibility of winning. Bob was paying her and I was handicapped from wearing Andrew's Cossack hat. Andrew, must have bought it at a Moscow flea market. It had long flaps to cover the ears giving me an appearance similar to Walt Disney's Goofy. It also was continually shedding large clumps of fur.

Radka showed us many of the tourist highlights of Prague and accompanied us to several restaurants noted for Czech cuisine. It was an elegant few days, resting from our flight, staying in a fine hotel, using their exercise, and steam rooms, and touring with Radka. Conversion work continued to be neglected

On Saturday, February 4th Bob and I flew to Budapest. There we met Dottie and her husband, Dr. George Cunningham, a doctor in the US Army and Bob's brother-in-law. They were stationed in Frankfort and he and Dottie flew to Budapest to tour with us. Budapest is a great city for tourists with many beautiful vistas on the Danube river. Bob arranged guides and a van that would accommodate all of us. Some tours I skipped as I used the time to fine-tune two lectures that Bruce had scheduled for me to do in Tirgu Mures, Romania.

Monday, February 6, Bob and I left Budapest via a small prop plane for a 45 minute flight to Cluj, Romania. We were met by Bruce and several volunteers from Bruce's Livada Orphan Care ministry in the mission van. Bruce drove the 1 1/2 hours to Tirgu Mures in a snow storm. He stopped periodically to show us scenic views and once to take our picture with some drunk gypsies in a horse drawn cart. The population of Tirgu Mures was about 100,000 and I figured Bob and I were going to take a big step down from our Prague/Budapest accommodations.

However, Bruce checked us into the one year old Hotel Concordia which, though small, had all attributes of the big city fine hotels. That night we had dinner at a restaurant with Bruce, his wife Catherine and their two adopted Romanian sons, Sam and Charlie.

Tirgu Mures, Romania

It was a beautiful night. The downtown, consisting of several Medieval buildings, was blanketed in snow. There was no traffic, the night was clear except for periodic snow flurries. The scene reminded me of a Christmas card. Throughout my stay in Tirgi Mures I had a sense of peacefulness. The Romanian people were so overtly pro-American and hospitable, the thought occurred, "I could live in a place like this."

However, all was not peaches and cream in Romania. For example when Bruce changed an American dollar he received 30,000 Lei. Run away inflation was not the only example of Romania's struggle to rise from third world status. The next morning Bruce picked us up to visit some of Livada's projects. Our first stop was Ludus Children's Home. It housed 200 children ages 6 - 19 in an institutional setting. Most of the children had been there all of their lives. The building and interior reminded me of the Texas state hospitals of the 1960's The rooms and hallways were dark and dingy with a prison-like atmosphere. When we entered we were mobbed by children starved for attention, affection, and stimulation. They were all desperate to touch and talk to us.

A nurse met with us and explained that the conditions in the Ludus institution were very bad. She said gangs roamed the halls at night and they terrorized and sexually assaulted boys and girls. Bruce's ministry was helping arrange transfer of children from the Ludus Institution into community and faith based living arrangements.

The most fortunate were placed in one of the three group homes Livada had built that were managed by a trained Christian staff, many being young dedicated Christians from the US. The three Livada homes could take care of only 60 children. There were 200 children housed at Ludus. which was one of nine orphanages Livada was attempting to serve in the Turga Mures area. There were similar needs all over Romania. One wonders how Romania came to have so many orphans housed in institutions. This is how it was explained to me:

Romania is still suffering the impact of the 1965-1989 rule of a brutal and misguided dictator, Nicolae Ceausescu. Ceausescu, faced with an economically floundering country, concluded the problem stemmed from an inadequate number of young workers and that this could be solved by increasing the Romanian birth rate. He initiated financial incentives for having children. The result was that there were thousands of children born to mothers who had no means to financially support them. These women abandoned the children to the care of the government and Ceausescu began to build and fill institutions with them.

Thinking that a germ-free, quiet environment was of primary importance, government programs were initiated that kept infants restrained in beds with little social interaction. Such emotional deprivation can cause children to be physically and intellectually delayed. The government response to these unhealthy infants was to give the sick children injections using inadequately sterilized needles resulting in a high incidence of AIDS. The cumulative result of such errors was the mob that Bob and I encountered at Ludus. The rein of Ceausescu ended in 1989 by a Romanian uprising when he and his wife were executed.

After our morning at Ludus we visited the Livada administrative offices and met many of the impressive staff. I was assigned a translator. Ironically his name was "Dan Myers," spelled in Romanian "Dan Maier" The plan was for me to give two lectures, one on "Dealing With Severe Behavior Problems" to the Livada staff and the other at Dimitri Cantemir University to their psychology students and staff on- "Psychiatric Management of Institutional Trauma in Children." The remainder of our time Bob and I would spend visiting the Livada group homes with the thought being I would be available for consultation in regard to difficult child behavior management issues.

At this point Bob announced that he quit! The Ludus group home was his limit. He had seen all he wanted to see of Livada orphans. He said, "Dan can do whatever he wants to do but I am not going with him." He said he was going to hire a driver, a guide, find a real estate agent and the remainder of his time in Romania he intended to look for good buys in Romanian real estate and be a tourist.

The Romania trip was not evolving the way I had planned, particularly in regard to my convert-Bob endeavor. The first week of the trip I had been too busy enjoying being a fat-cat tourist in Prague and Budapest and the second part looked like Bruce was going to take every second I was in Romania squeezing all the child psychiatry I ever learned out of me.

"God's ways are not our ways." Bob asked Bruce if he would help him locate a driver and guide. Bruce responded that he had some time available and he would be happy to drive Bob around. Perfect, Bob would be spending several days with a real minister. I felt sure God had planned it that way. Bruce would be much better at converting Bob than I could have ever hoped.

Dan Maier, my Romanian translator, picked me up each morning and accompanied me to a group home or to the location where I would be lecturing.

At the group home I would be introduced to their problem children followed by a review of the case and discussion of feasible approaches. Although most of the children had experienced enough environmental stress, abandonment, and loss to account for their symptoms, some showed evidence of other psychiatric illnesses, likely related to genetic factors. Romania did not allow importation or use of stimulant medications to treat ADHD but there were alternative medications that were being under utilized. Although the newer antipsychotic medications were not available they had access to most of the older medications and these sometimes were being over used.

Behavioral management issues were complicated and discussion of the psychodynamics between patients and staff was useful. Discouragement and burnout of staff was an important factor, and the staff greatly appreciated and was relieved when I could confirm that their efforts were therapeutic and helpful. A few of the children were clearly incorrigible and presented an ongoing risk to the other residents and staff. Time was devoted to finding ways for their transfer to other satisfactory living situations.

After one of my lectures, Bruce and Bob picked me up and we drove 50 miles to visit Transylvania to tour Count Dracula's castle. There I learned that he was infamous not for being a vampire but for impaling people on his castle gates he disagreed with.

On the way back to Tirgu Mures I became aware of how excited and joyful both Bob and Bruce appeared. I looked carefully to see if either showed a halo but none was seen. We stopped at a local bank as we entered Tirgu Mures. Bob and Bruce were meeting there with an attorney to sign some papers. It turned out Bob had convinced Bruce to trade in a Romanian lot that he owned in order to go into business with Bob and some other US investors to buy Romanian real estate. While I had been doing my consulting they had already bought three properties. Bruce hadn't converted Bob; Bob had converted Bruce!

That is not to say that all religious value was lost. "God's ways are not our ways." Who knows what will be the ultimate value of that trip for Bob, Bruce, me, or Livada? I do know that subsequently Bob paid for an outstanding young man who Bob was mentoring to go to Romania and join the Livada staff.

Bob and I left Tirgu Mures Saturday February 11th at 3:30 AM in a heavy snowstorm for our short flight from Cluj. In Budapest Bob changed all our scheduled flights so we flew to London's Heathrow airport then Chicago where Bob flew back to Tennessee and I to Dallas. Kathy picked me up at 7:00 PM at DFW. I had been awake for 29 hours but never found the time to try to convert Bob.

Reflections on Romania:
Secular-

The trip to Romania was an education. I didn't know there was an Eastern European country that spoke a Latin language or that the Romanian language is so similar to original Latin.

The problems of the Romanian orphans were unknown to me and I knew nothing of the dictator Nicolae Ceausescu. It softens my heart to learn of others' needs and motivates me to help.

The trip was an excellent opportunity to spend time and share an adventure with my cousin, Bob Crosby.

The trip satisfied my curiosity about how my Bible study friend Jim Vandemeer's daughter was doing as a missionary in a far away country and permitted me to report her accomplishments and well being to her parents.

Theological-

God's way is not necessarily our way. What good will come of this trip, only God knows

The trip showed me how the power of a loving, caring, Christian relationship can bring about improvement in situations and illnesses that seem hopeless. Repeatedly, the children I interviewed in the group homes demonstrated improving mental health where I would have predicted a less favorable prognosis

Someone once told me, it is hard to guide a car that is not moving. The lesson is when confronted by a problem of great magnitude one should go ahead and get started doing what you can and, with prayer, the Holy Spirit can magnify your effort and result.

A similar lesson is taught when Jesus fed 4000 people with only a few fish and loves of bread. Matthew 15:35-36 "He told the crowd to sit down on the ground. Then he took the seven loaves and the fish, and when he had given thanks, he broke them and gave them to the disciples, and they in turn to the people. They all ate and were satisfied." Jesus told the disciples to start with the few fish and loaves that they had and begin to feed the people. He did not tell them to wait until they had enough food to begin.

The Christian workers at Livada have begun to do what they can with 60 beds when 1,000s are needed. Since Bob's and my trip in 2006, Livada has built another group home so that adds 20 more beds. Other agencies and the government have provided hundreds more. Ludus and the other government institutions housing Romanian orphans have now been closed. It all started with Livada and others doing the best they could with what little they had.

Being Called To China?

After returning from both Cuba and Romania, I was restless. It bothered me that I could see little indications that either of the two trips had accomplished what I had hoped. I don't know what I expected, but it probably had to do with my disappointment that my two books on Biblical parenting had not sold better or been reprinted. It seemed to me that the Holy Spirit had gone to a whole lot of trouble to guide and protect me on these trips for a result that to me was not that impressive. (In retrospect, it is frightening to realize how I had the audacity to fault God for not following **my** plan.)

Having a strong feeling that God had a purpose for me, but wondering if I was on the right path, I wanted to know God's will. I searched scripture for answers. Job 37:5, "God's voice thunders in marvelous ways. He does great things beyond our understanding." As I was in this process of further study, I began to sense signs that God was calling me to China.

It started by my being invited to speak to a class of Mandarin speaking Christians at Highland Park Presbyterian Church. This group was the nucleus of Reverend Ben Wang's Chinese Church plant. The group was interested in learning my views about Chinese parents applying American child rearing techniques. They also had questions about the controversial parenting recommendations expressed in the popular book, The Battle Hymn of the Tiger Mother by Amy Chua. Several members of the class suggested I go to China to lecture about Biblical parenting.

China missionary, Mike Crutcher and his wife, Cristal, returned to Dallas about that time. They spontaneously invited me to visit them in Zhengzhou. Through Ben and Esther Wang I received an invitation to conduct a seminar about Biblical parenting at Root publishing house in Beijing.

Subsequently, I was contacted by two Chinese physicians working at UT Southwestern Medical school. Both requested that I allow them to shadow me in my child psychiatry practice and both were willing to help edit my Biblical parenting book to make it more appropriate and useful to Chinese parents. Mike Crutcher also invited me to speak at an expat Church in Beijing.

It is tedious to make plans to do a lecture tour in China as communication must be carefully worded and disguised. There are two main utilized paths in China for pursuing a Christian religious life. There is the official Communist sanctioned and controlled Protestant Church, known as "The Three-Self Patriotic Movement." This title affirms that the churches must be self-administrated (no foreign control), self- supported (no foreign funding) and self- propagating (no outside evangelizing.) The other path is the Underground Church.

In 1949 Mao Zedong defeated Chiang Kai-shek and established the People's Republic of China, a Communist government. Chiang Kai-shek and his National party fled to Taiwan. Initially Mao Zedong closed all churches and banned foreign missionaries. Despite persecution from the government, underground Churches flourished. In response Mao Zedong established the Communist government conceived and controlled Three -Self Patriotic Movement of the Protestant Church.

Initially, there were marked differences in the character and theology of these two religious paths. The Underground Church continued the fundamental theology that had been taught by Western missionaries. The Communist sanctioned Church altered the theology to bring it more in sync with Communist doctrine. For example preaching the Trinity was not allowed, there could be no religious training of children, nor any evangelizing. Participants in the Underground church were viewed as enemies of the state, and there has been ongoing persecution of it's members and leaders. However, over the last 70 years there has been much integration of traditional Western Protestant theology into the Government Controlled Church. Despite this, the Underground Church is reluctant to come under the mantle of the Three-Self Patriotic Movement, as it fears that if members identify themselves they may be arrested, or that the government will over-control their ministry. This means that they practice their religion in secret, something the communist Party does not tolerate.

Such cloak and dagger intrigue made it exceedingly difficult for me to understand or plan my options in visiting. For example, I was cautioned about using certain words in email communication. Reportedly, all internet activity is monitored by the

Communist government and certain words or patterns will trigger a more intensive review.

Except for the Beijing publisher's invitation, most of the contact with me was coming from the underground church. Their material usually would not contain specific dates, locations, or topics. Even the Beijing publisher, who appeared to be working with government approval, seemed to be sensitive to the risk of providing too much information. My talk would be in seminar format, but no one informed me who the audience would be, or for what length of time I should prepare my topics. I was given no seminar address and, only when I was contacted at my hotel the night before my talk did I learn that someone was coming to pick me up.

I had decided to go to China primarily because of all of the signs I saw signaling that the trip was God's will. However, several weeks before departure I was asked to present at Discussion "C," an adult Highland Park Presbyterian Church Sunday school class. For my topic I chose " Finding God's Will," hoping that research and discussion from teaching the class might help me be more confident about making the China trip.

Research revealed a book written by Bruce Waltke, a professor of the Old Testament and Hebrew, titled, Finding the Will of God. He proposed a formula for determining what is God's will. Waltke says when a thought comes into your mind as your heart's desire, don't trust "signs" that God confirms your thought. He says signs are the least trustworthy. If Satan should be trying to deceive you, signs would be the way he would proceed. The better approach is to look to Scripture to make sure that there is no Biblical contraindication. If there is no Biblical reason to question your intention, Waltke then recommends that you pray for guidance, then run your idea past respected church members. If they concur with your plan and you continue to feel strongly, you should proceed. Always be aware that God's providence may trump the plans of man. Whether you are actually doing God's will may be suspected by the way things turn out but I suppose if you want to be sure, you will have to wait to check it out in Heaven.

After reading Finding God's Will, I discounted most of the very persuasive signs that encouraged my China trip. Waltke's formula was reviewed and discussed during my presentation to the

HPPC Sunday School class. This class included several Deacons and Elders, and many of the members were serious Bible students. The class qualified as a "respected group of Church members" Waltke said to consult. The class discussion confirmed my plans met Waltke's criteria.

One clear blessing and possible sign of God's approval for my China trip was that my grandson, 21 year old Barret Howell happened to be on spring break at the University of Texas on the same days I was scheduled to be in China. He unhesitatingly cancelled going to his senior fraternity beach party and accepted my invitation to accompany me to China. Definitely a Godsend was Mike Crutcher, missionary living in Zhengzhou, China, arranging to shepherd us once we arrived in China. Mike and I talked a couple of times on Skype prior to the trip but the connections were never perfect and security prevented Mike from being clear and precise.

Mike sent me an email giving the name of the hotel where he would be staying in Beijing with instructions that we were to meet him Sunday, March 11 in Beijing at Capital Community Church, an expat church. My Dallas assistant, stepdaughter, Heather Roberts, selected our hotel from the internet attempting to find one that was in close proximity to Capital Community Church. My understanding was that a delegation of underground pastors were planning to meet with me while I was in Beijing.

Our schedule for China was so vague and unspecified it was requiring a jump of faith to proceed. Barret had little awareness of the uncertainties of the trip and was happy as a clam. Barret's confidence that all was carefully arranged left no room for me to let him down. Whatever, I was going to make the jump.

Barret and I left Dallas at 7:00 AM via American Airlines on March 9, 2012. In Seattle we changed to Heinam Airline, arriving in Beijing at 5:00 PM Saturday, March 10. Heinam airline was economy class and I do mean economy! No-frills didn't bother Barret. On landing in Beijing, to my surprise, there was no security check. We went directly from the gate it the taxi area where I showed the name of our hotel written in Mandarin to a driver who spoke no English. He took my paper with the hotel name and motioned for us to get in. There was steel mesh separating the driver from the back seat. We rode about 30 minutes when the driver stopped at a street that was barricaded. He motioned us out of the taxi, pointed down the street and drove off.

By this time it was dark and there was nothing in view that resembled a hotel. We began walking down the street that was barricaded, dragging our baggage. There were a few parked cars but no moving traffic. Every few blocks we would come across a small unlighted booth in the middle of the street that housed a policeman. None spoke English nor could give us any direction for finding our hotel.

Soon we began to pass huge statues on the side walks , most were surreal and of grotesque subjects. For example one was of a threatening 30 foot tall Mao Zedong. Another was of a scene of over sized snarling wolves!

Walking through the Art District in Beijing (the night before we stumbled on this in the dark while lost and looking for our hotel).

Eventually we found a few restaurants open. I would inquire if anyone spoke English. We never found a person who said they did. However, we did find a few that seemed to recognize the Chinese character symbolizing the name of our hotel. From these people we would be pointed in various directions, never giving us confidence we were heading correctly. Then just when we felt we would be in the street all night, we looked up and there was the name of our hotel written on a small insignificant looking door. We opened it and walked into the modern, luxurious lobby of the "Grace" Hotel. (another sign?)

It was a great relief to talk to the young Chinese girls working at the front desk who spoke perfect English. I gave them the name and address of the expat Church, Capital Community, where we were to meet Mike Crutcher, the missionary. One of the reasons we had picked our hotel was that it appeared to be within walking distance to the church, but it was a thirty minute taxi ride from our hotel.

Sunday was a beautiful cold morning in Beijing and during the night 4 inches of snow had fallen. There was no sign of pollution in the sky. However, the snow was gray.

There were about 400 people attending Capital Community Church. It had the feeling of a contemporary US service. The sermon was in English and the pastor and his wife, Tom and Iris Lowder, had previously been on the staff at Highland Park Presbyterian Church in Dallas. The Chinese government does not allow Chinese citizens to attend ex-pat churches. Everyone must have a foreign passport.

It had been my understanding that the next Sunday, March 18th, I was invited to speak to a Sunday school class. During the service, Tom announced I would be the guest speaker to the congregation. Speaking with Tom after the service, I learned I would be expected to speak for 30 min and that I should come to the church 30 minutes early to work out details.

The Lowders arranged a driver to take Barret and me to tour the Great Wall of China. We walked about a mile along the wall. Most of it was uphill and the portion we were walking along was in poor repair. The finishing bricks were no longer in place and each step was either up or down irregularly stacked 3 foot rectangular stones. The saving grace was that at the end of our walk there was a commercial toboggan ride that could be used to get back to ground level. That too was a little more than I expected. I found myself applying the brake so frequently that Barret continually ran up against me from behind.

We learned that the area we were in the night before was an art district housing an Art University. No car traffic was allowed in the art district The grotesque statues of the night before were student projects and were not nearly as fearful in the daytime.

The Great China Wall trip was one of the few times in China when I faced the disadvantage of being 75 years old. Most of the time the Chinese women were so respectful and accommodating I sometimes suffered the illusion their interest was romantic. This was particularly noticeable following a lecture I gave at Henan Provincial People's Hospital in Zhengzhou to about 200 pediatricians and neurologists. There a fifty year old female pediatric neurologist stuck herself tightly next to me and appeared ready to fight any one who had the thought to displace her. She scrambled to make sure she was in the back seat of our car beside me and at the dinner in our honor she was intent on seeing that I had everything I could want. She initiated toasts given in my honor. By the end of the evening I was feeling a little sorry for her because she was so smitten by me.

Perspective readjustment came when we were going back to the car and she had again attached herself to my arm. Insight occurred when we went to step over a curb and she pushed up on my arm to help me over a three inch step. So much for romantic illusion. She was just being very kind to an old man.

On our return to the hotel, I had a call from Tommy, a Chinese executive from Root publishing. He said he would pick me up the next morning to drive us to their offices where the seminar would be conducted. Tommy, who spoke good English, came to our hotel early Monday morning. Barret and I rode with him in a taxi to Root Publishing. On the way I learned Root publishes a monthly magazine devoted to child rearing. They also have a division that trains and hires teacher to go into rural areas to meet with families and advise them about parenting. These teachers were to be my audience at the seminar.

Tommy took us to lunch in a Japanese restaurant located in a modern glass office building where the seminar would be held. From my reading I had the idea that the Chinese have contempt for the Japanese because of atrocities by the Japanese when they occupied China during World War II. This is another example of how in China things are often not what you expect.

Mike Crutcher did not go with us to Root publishing. He gave me the impression that this might present some risk to him. He did not explain further. He and his wife Cristal are continually cautious about anything that brings them to the attention of the government and could jeopardize their stay in the country.

After lunch we went up to the 10th floor offices of Root Publishing. It was nice and neat but showed little indication of being a high powered publishing company. There was a conference room with about 40 teachers, mostly women. I was introduced to my translator, a pleasant and capable young woman named "Hope."

The reason for the seminar and their interest in my book was that when the Communists took control of China in 1949 traditional Chinese parenting methods and parenting instruction taught by missionaries were replaced with Communist principles and regulations. Time has shown the limitations and ineffectiveness of parenting by government regulation. Replacing thousands of years of Chinese parenting traditions with untested new Communist childrearing theory is not working out. Children grown into adults guided by Communist doctrine suffered from compromised character and morality. Communist leaders recognized the political and business disadvantage of having a reputation for being untrustworthy. The child rearing wisdom found in the Bible was being considered as a better model. This helped me to understand why so many doors were opening up to me in Communist venues. However, being a Communist, atheist country they preferred to ignore religious ramifications such as the existence of God and Jesus. My talks during the China visit, to the best I could determine, were not censored and the information was well received.

The Root Publishing teachers who attended my seminar on Biblical parenting asked many thoughtful questions and my impression was that the material in the book was helpful to them. It seemed like God had gotten on board with my plan that my book would be published in Mandarin. However, Tommy and the other administrative staff choose not to publish my book. They said it had too many references to the Bible.

Their caution was well advised. Although most of the administrative staff at Root said they were Christians, in China the political climate can change quickly and the consequences can be significant. Something that is acceptable today could draw an arrest or prison term tomorrow.

That night, back at the Grace hotel, I had a surprising call from Mike Crutcher. Mike had received an email from a businessman from Taiwan, John Chen, who said he had been meeting with the president of Yanjing Theological Seminary in Beijing. She told him she would like to invite Dr. Myers to present a seminar to Yanjing Seminary students and staff on Wednesday morning, March 13. Also the Seminary had planned a dinner in our honor the evening of Tuesday March 12th.

I can understand how the previous paragraph may seem disjointed and out of context. If so, maybe the reader will appreciate how in China I was largely in the dark about what would come next and what forces were directing us. Keep in mind the saying, " In China things are not as they seem." What does one present when, out of the blue, he is asked to speak about Biblical Parenting in a Seminary controlled and taught by Communists who are atheists?

Tuesday morning the 12th, nothing was on my schedule so Mike escorted us through the Forbidden City. We were tourists. John Chen's driver picked us up at our hotel in a new Black Mercedes Sedan. From that afternoon until our departure Monday, March 19, John Chen put himself, his hospitality, car, and his driver completely at our disposal. His wife, ShaoLee, was with him and both attended all of our activities in Beijing. It was never explained to me how we merited such attention and expense.

John Chen is from Taiwan and comes to Dallas on business enough to maintain a Dallas apartment. John showed me some pictures of his father with Chiang Kai-shek. He said his father was a member of Chiang Kai-shek's cabinet. Another example of how nothing in China is the way it seems. Having a Taiwan business-man with strong connections to Chiang Kai-shek being our patron on mainland China seemed incongruent.

Later that evening I received a telephone call saying that all plans to meet with the underground pastors had been cancelled. Since I was now working with the Communist approved church they felt it was not safe to meet with me.

After the morning tour of the Forbidden City, Mike Crutch-er, Barret and I were taken to Yanjing Theological Seminary. After seeing the facility and chatting with a few students and staff, I met with my interpreter, Dr. Jungang. He was a small Chinese man who seemed very nervous during our meeting. At the time I had the feeling that he was carefully checking what I might be going to say the next day. In retrospect, I believe he was nervous as he was not routinely a translator and he was concerned he might mess it up. Also, if you are a communist working in a Christian seminary and your boss, Ying Gao a Central Committee member of the Communist Party, would be in the audience, it would keep you nervous!

The Seminary has a sign in front with it's motto, "Freedom Through Truth For Service." The seminary offers a four year Bachelor of Theology degree. There are 124 full time students.

Dr. Myers standing in front of Beijing Yanjing Seminary
before speaking to students and staff on "Biblical Parenting."

The sanctuary where I spoke was very similar to those in US
churches. Throughout the campus are statues depicting Biblical
scenes. The one I most remember was of Jesus washing a disci-
ple's feet.

Standing: Mike Crutcher, John Chen, Barret Howell, Dr. Jungang
Seated: Dan, President Gao, ShaoLee Chen

That night we had a dinner in the private dining room of a Chinese restaurant. I was seated as the honored guest with fish soup in front of me with the head of the fish pointing toward me as is the tradition.

Conversation was in English. Everyone seemed to choose their words carefully and there was a mild feeling of suspicion. None of it seemed to bother Barret who ate like he was starving. There were many courses and the meal was elegantly served.

The next day we were picked up by John and his driver and arrived at the seminary around noon. The academic Dean, Chen Xun invited us to his office for a tea ceremony. This began with his getting out a decorative tea table and tea box designed for the tea ceremony. Dr. Xun carefully choose the type of tea he wanted and explained the history and rationale for its serving.

The teas came in a small square foil wrapping, was opened and the tea leaves were soaked with hot water from a special pot. The liquid tea was then transferred multiple times into colorful small Chinese designed bowls until he felt it was ready to be drunk. Only a small portion was served to each of us. It tasted fine, but not being an experienced hot tea drinker, I probably didn't appreciate it as much as I should have.

Following the tea ceremony, we went downstairs to the sanctuary where I was introduced to the audience of students and faculty. I was presented a crystal statue with engraved logos in re-membrance of my visit and lecture.

My lecture on Biblical based parenting was translated with some difficulty by Dr. Jungang. He was assisted occasionally by ChaoLee Chen who was sitting in the front row of pews. There were questions and discussion following my 45 minute lecture. President Gao was in the audience smiling and nodding in agree-ment with some of my comments.

After the lecture Mike Crutcher, Barret and I proceeded to the airport and then flew to Zhengzhou via Air China. The plane was not as opulent as most American planes but it was neat, clean, and the crew was courteous and efficient. Zhengzhou (pronounced: "Jung Joe" is a town in Central China. I knew nothing about it, even though its population is seven million.

We were met in Zhengzhou by one of Mike's Chinese friends who drove us to Mike's and Cristal's apartment. Mike and Cristal live in an apartment on the very edge of the Henan Agricultural University campus where Cristal teaches conversational English. Their apartment shares a common wall with the hotel where we stayed. Their apartment , from the outside seemed rundown and needed painting, However, inside it was very nice with hardwood floors, nice kitchen and a study.

The Crutchers don't have a car and there are many parked bicycles in the area of their apartment. Henan University has over 20,000 students. They are about 1/2 block from the university and a busy intersection. All types of shopping is within walking or biking range.

The hotel we stayed in was a typical Chinese hotel known as hard-bed hotels. The room was adequate but there were no mattresses and the sheets and blankets went directly on what appeared to be thin bed pads on top of plywood. Surprisingly, I slept comfortably and soundly. The girls at the front desk were nothing like the girls at the Grace hotel in Beijing. These front desk girls were dressed in the padded uniforms commonly worn by Chinese soldiers. They spoke no English.

The price was right. We had prepaid for our room but there was a commotion when I tried to check out. If Cristal hadn't happened to come by we might still be there, I had taken a match box from the room and they were not going to let me leave until it was accounted for.

On Thursday March 15, Mike had arranged for me to speak at Henan Provincial Peoples Hospital where about 200 pediatricians and neurologists were in attendance. Thankfully, I had my laptop and was able to adapt a previous talk on college suicide to present to the Zhengzhou doctors. Suicides have been increasing in Chinese university students.

Following the talk there was another dinner in our honor. Barret wasn't in attendance. Cristal had arranged for Barret to teach her conversational English class at Henan Agriculture University.

Barret showed slides and spoke about being a senior at the University of Texas. The students loved it. They held a raffle to see which 10 students would be permitted to take him to dinner that night. While I was looking at the fish head looking back at me, Barret was singing the Eyes of Texas in a Chinese karaoke bar.

Barret teaching in Zhengzhou

The next morning Barret gave another lecture and afterwards Mike Crutcher and I visited The Swallows Nest, an orphan's home for children with disabilities. That night night Cristal, Mike and I went to a great hot pot restaurant as Barret had again been auctioned off for karaoke.

Saturday we rode the high speed train rather than a plane back to Beijing. It traveled at 150 miles per hour. It was comfortable and we made the 500 miles back to Beijing in three and one half hours. The towns we passed all had pollution worse than Beijing.

Sunday, John Shen picked us up and took us to Capital Community Church and he and ShaoLee stayed and heard me give my first sermon. God only knows how it went. Barret said it went well. By that point I was ready to let God take over. Usually I err on being overly prepared and too much in control.

An interesting phenomena occurred during my "sermon." While in the mist of relating my experience of hypnotizing Ann-Lawson and her impact on my Christian walk, a thought as clear as a voice came to me. It was that Ann had struggled to live and endured her cancer pain to have more time to impact me.

That evening John and ShaoLee took us to a Beijing restaurant famous for Peking Duck. It also featured a whole fried fish (with it's head pointed toward me) that was marvelous. Following desert John drove us to a special entrance he knew at the Forbidden City and it was beautiful to see it lit at night.

We left Beijing the next day heading back to the US on Hainan Airlines.

Reflections on China:

Secular - It was great to have my grandson Barret Howell with me. His ready acceptance of my invitation was the culminating stroke that persuaded me to make the trip to China. He was a great help. He handled our luggage, and without him I would have gotten lost more. Barret was our GPS. I enjoyed his company and I felt very good about providing him the opportunity for such a unique perspective of China.

The trip gave me a hands-on appreciation of some of China's complex governing problems that are increasingly in the news and impacting the world. There is no better way to become enlightened than to experience a country first hand.

It was even better to see and appreciate the missionary work that Cristal and Mike are doing. I was privileged to visit them.

Theological - China forced me to realize that it is not necessary, good, or possible to control one's destiny. Repeatedly, planned activities in China never developed, or were changed. The lectures and presentations I gave in China were the most effective when I let the Holy Spirit lead me. It allowed the focus to be on the message rather on the quality of the presentation.

China showed me that things may not be what they seem and it is best to be patient before judging others.

The often but slowly learned lesson that God's ways are not our ways was demonstrated again in China.

Flunking Retirement

When Barret and I returned from China I cut my practice down to three days a week. Full retirement was on Kathy's and my mind. One afternoon a stranger knocked on our office door and offered to buy the log cabin, letting me decide the terms. Six months later I was retired from the active clinical practice of psychiatry and had rented a small office in Preston Center, 0.8 miles from our home. Having the office gave me a place to go while Kathy and Lacy used our home as their sometimes real estate office. I hired my stepdaughter, Heather, to work part time for me as I sorted through options for staying busy.

My plan evolved as follows: I would take one year to pursue leads in China that seemed promising for having my Biblical parenting book published in Mandarin. Six months later, I had exhausted these leads and I decided to close the door on China. I had done all I knew to do. Despite encouraging signs, it didn't appear that publishing Biblical Parenting, Chinese Version was in God's plan. Maybe God intended for me to play more Golf

Golf

Increasing the times I played golf was a help but my inability to improve my game was a continuous frustration. Our golf group, Doyle Traylor, Roy Chapman, Tony Stevens and sometimes Moody Alexander played once or twice a week. My childhood friend, Tommy Flood, would sometime drive down from Austin and back just to join the fun of whipping me at golf.

True to my basic personality, I never gave up and always tried harder, which everyone knows makes you score worse. Not that I didn't devise ways to have some revenge. By creative ways of betting I partially compensated for my inability to play decent golf. A few times I even won some money.

But the sweetest revenge of all came as a result of unplanned circumstances providing the ingredients for a great practical joke. It happened to fall on Doyle Traylor, a legendary Baylor University quarterback who because of multiple injuries, we call the greatest quarterback who never played for Baylor. He is a slight curmudgeon but good-natured and fun to tease.

Our foursome is waiting on the number four tee box at Cedar Creek Golf course in Oak Cliff. About 75 yards away from the tee box is number three green. Fifty yards behind the green is an iron fence with a gate separating the golf course from the street. In-between the green and the fence is a portable restroom. Doyle decides this is a good opportunity to take a leak so he heads toward the porto-potty. I decide that Doyle has a good idea so, unbeknownst to Doyle, I am right behind him. When he is about half-way to the porto-potty a large clean-out truck stops at the gate, a helper opens the gate and the truck with its backup warning bell sounding begins to slowly back down toward the porto-potty. Doyle picks up his pace, estimating he has time to get in and out of the portable restroom before it is serviced or taken away.

He quickly opens the door and goes inside. By this time the truck backup bell is so loud it sounds like the driver is coming through the porto-potty door. At that instant I reach the backside of the port potty, grab both sides as high as I can reach and begin to rock it side to side.

Doyle begins shouting "Whoa" and "Hold On" certain he had been picked up and was about to be dropped into a shit tank. The door swings open and out he runs, eyes big as saucers, fly unzipped and wet Bermuda shorts. The rest of us are rolling on the ground laughing. The problem about practical jokes is that "what goes around, comes around." I have had to keep a cautious eye on Doyle ever since.

Pecan Valley

In September 2012, Heather, my assistant and stepdaughter, brought to my attention an internet ad seeking a child psychiatrist to work in a mental health clinic in Cleburne, Texas. This was only 15 miles from our second home at the Retreat, a golfing resort between Cleburne and Glenrose, Texas.

I stopped by the Cleburne Pecan Valley Clinic to discuss the possibility of my working part time. The clinical director had previously been a Baptist minister and there was an immediate meeting of our minds. He basically said, "We will work out whatever you want to do."

Over the next 18 months my job evolved to playing golf at the Retreat on Sundays, spending the night, working Mondays in Cleburne at the Pecan Valley Child Clinic driving back to Dallas and doing telemedicine for Pecan Valley two other days of the week. The work was rewarding as the patients and families had no child psychiatrists in their area and they were very appreciative of my availability. However, telemedicine was a new experience for Pecan Valley and me. The infrastructure for delivery of service had not evolved, and there were many administrative frustrations for everyone. Converting to digital records was a challenge and I found myself working longer hours to compensate for my slow typing.. During this time, my back problems worsened and a five month leave of absence was arranged in April 2015 to allow me to obtain medical or surgical treatment.

.

God Has Other Plans For Me

Several neurosurgeons were consulted about my back. The consensus was that my diagnosis was spinal stenosis limited to L4, L5 vertebra, and that the lesion was surgically correctible. All consultants confirmed that the MRIs showed the stenosis was progressing and likely would continue to do so. I was scheduled for a lumbar laminectomy on June 6, 2015 at Zale Lipshy Hospital in Dallas.

On the morning of May 30th, I took my temperature. I had put myself on antibiotics several days previously because of symptoms of a cold. My temperature was 101 degrees. Being concerned that the antibiotic I had prescribed may not be the best selection and that my cold could be developing into something serious enough to interfere with back surgery, I sought a better medical opinion. I drove to the emergency room at Dallas' Clements Hospital and requested a chest Xray and to see a doctor.

While I was in the emergency room, I went into respiratory arrest and was intubated. Three days later I woke up, in the ICU on life support surrounded by medical staff and family who had been called. The doctors concluded I had a severe viral pneumonia that had also affected my heart. Cardiac cauterization while I was unconscious showed my heart output was only 20%, barely enough to support life. A heart team headed by Dr. James de Lemos of UT Southwestern Medical School provided superb medical care. Friends and family, mobilized hundreds of prayer warriors to pray for my health. I was discharged from Clements Hospital June 8th, and was readmitted on August 6, 2015 to have a cardiac pacemaker and defibrillator implanted in my chest.

On November 9th, 2015 I underwent successful back surgery for spinal stenosis.

God's Hand

When someone reviews the important events that shaped his/her life, you would hope it correlated with a thoughtful, planned course. In my case, a map for redemption was never on my mind. Luck or Something Else protected and directed me from unseen dangers and from getting so far in the wrong direction I would be forever lost. I have come to believe that Something Else was the hand of God. The following are some of the guides and markers along this road, in retrospect, that seem important:

- A grandmother from my birth directing me to medicine
- A mother giving me perpetual optimism
- A father who instilled respect for authority
- Surviving childhood brushes with life threatening events
    - Compressed skull fracture
    - Snake killing shotgun accident
    - Playing "chicken" driving car
    - Lived through foolish behaviors in Mexico
- God's presence felt when answered child's prayer for snow
- Gift of stamina for athletics and practicing medicine
- University of Texas on a football scholarship
- Avoided football concussion syndrome
- Early admission to medical school
- Army orders to Vietnam changed to instructor in Texas
- Out-of-body-experience during a heat stroke
- Prayer relief during painful divorce
- Impact of treating Ann Lawson's cancer pain
- Finding and marrying Kathy
- Receiving a Bible from Kathy's sister and brother in law
- Interest in historical fiction switched to religious literature
- Developed a passion for Bible Study
- Compulsion to write a book on Biblical parenting
- Mission trip to Cuba
- Deacon at Highland Park Presbyterian Church
- Humanitarian and lecture trip to Romania
- Guest lecturer to numerous Sunday school classes
- Lecturing on Biblical Parenting in China
- Drove self to ER to get a chest Xray for suspected bronchitis

- Respiratory arrest and heart failure occurred while in the ER
- Put on life support and treated for viral pneumonia.
    Prayer support from many.
    9 months later heart and lungs normal
- Tour of Holy Land led by Dr. Jim Denison

The list above is drawn primarily from the memoir portion of this book. There are hundreds of other events and persons that could have been listed as course changers in my life. For example, I had several people tell me, after Golden Rules For Parenting was published, and they learned I had become a Christian, that they had been praying for me for years.

From a secular point of view I am largely satisfied with my life. I wouldn't mind it continuing like this for a long time. Unfortunately, old age, doesn't give a secularist hope for the future. Jesus didn't encourage this position when He said in John 12:25, "Anyone who loves their life will lose it, while anyone who hates their life in this world will keep it for eternal life."

It takes my breath away to think how off track I lived much of my life and how dangerously I was playing with fire and brimstone. My rescue by God was not sought but I now realize and am grateful for His patience, persistence, protection and love.

Rushing To Redemption

Introduction

A good friend who read an earlier proof of <u>The Book of Dan</u> said, "Your memoir was interesting and entertaining. The apologetics portion is not funny and seems too directive and pushy."

He's right of course. However, my 79th birthday, speaking at three funerals and attending numerous others, have made me sensitive to the limits set by our earthly mortality. Dying doesn't seem that funny to me and what happens after that is even more serious!

Some people think after death nothing follows but a nice sound sleep. Consider this: Don't many people you know and respect, and billions of people who lived before you believe differently? French mathematician and philosopher, Blaise Pascal (1623-1662) suggested this wager, "Bet on God and you may gain eternal life. If you are wrong you are no worse off in death."

On December 2, 1978, while participating in a marathon race, a heat stroke caused me to have a near death experience. Not being a Christian at the time, floating comfortably apart from my body was given no religious significance. It did give me personal confirmation that some form of life will continue after we die.

Most of us recognize that the time we live on earth is relatively short. We carefully plan our human activity, trying to squeeze out the best from it while we are still living on earth. Few of us give the same attention to maximizing our life-after-death experience, even though it is said to continue for eternity.

In the Bible the apostles Peter and Paul describe our human body being like a tent where our spirit or soul lives during our life on earth.

Doctors never refer to there being a dead spirit or soul still inside a lifeless body. Scientific jargon is lost when we speak to the deceased's family. We refer to death with words such as "she has passed, he is no longer with us, she is gone," Our language reflects the universal understanding that when a human dies they actually leave their body and go to some other place. Many of us have seen persons near death speak to someone that others can-not see. The patient shows a peaceful countenance and seems to be preparing to join the person to whom they are speaking.

It is the body that is dead, not the person who lived in it. What remains is a lifeless tent that has no spark of the light that had shown before their soul left the body. My mother who died recently at one hundred years of age clearly exhibited this phenomena. She had expired two hours before my arrival at her bedside. It was shocking how clearly the body that remained no longer contained her. There was no sign she was in the tent.

Hundreds of people reporting, by way of the internet, leaving their lifeless body and observing it dispassionately as they float above their hospital bed confirm a phenomenon most doctors had recognized but have kept to themselves.

Intelligent Design

Even an informed atheist would give the "afterlife" serious thought. From a scientific, secular perspective it has become clear that when a person's body dies his spirit leaves and goes somewhere. If you agree, the next obstacle you will face is *intelligent design.* If a spirit leaves its body, where does it go and who directs this process?

A story is told of a scientist exploring an island that had never been visited by another human being. During his search, he comes across a pocket watch. As he pondered how the watch could exist on an uninhabited and unexplored island, he considers many possibilities. One option he does not consider is the watch had been formed by random collision of molecules. He accepts there had been a watchmaker.

A "watch" is infinitely simpler than the awe-inspiring exactness shown in a human chromosome. There is much scientific evidence that cellular life is far too complex to have evolved randomly. For a single cell to *spontaneously* mutate, and then by *natural selection* be formed into the billions of integrated cells that make up the organs and systems of the human body, is impossible regardless of how many billions of years you allow for those interactions to occur. Evolution within species is conceivable if one is describing how natural selection might favor the development of a bird with a longer beak. To use this reasoning to conclude how a human brain evolved seems preposterous.

Just as the scientist knew that a watchmaker existed, reason tells us that only a "maker" could create life. For millenniums people, awed by the beauty and precision of our universe, have called that maker "God." You probably know people you respect who believe in God.

How God created and maintains the universe is beyond our conception. NASA recently revised it's estimate of the universe size saying it now believed there are two trillion galaxies. Our Milky Way Galaxy is thought to contain 300 billion stars. If our intelligent design spirit, God, is able to balance and maintain the contents of His universe (86 trillion stars) it is easy to see how he could keep up with even the hairs on the heads of Earth's only seven billion inhabitants. (Luke 12: **6** Are not five sparrows sold for two pennies? Yet not one of them is forgotten by God. **7** Indeed, the very hairs of your head are all numbered. Don't be afraid; you are worth more than many sparrows.)

How this all fits together we will learn once we get to Heaven. What is important is that we confess that creation required intelligent design. Evolution is just one theory about the method God may have used to create the universe and life on earth. Evolution needs to be discussed further when it's claims challenge scripture to a degree that it turns people from God. Otherwise, if you have faith in what the Bible says, I wouldn't waste my time arguing with an evolutionist or trying to second guess God about his methods. When the end comes, if you believe in Jesus Christ as your Lord and Savior you should be as safe as you can be; believing in evolution should be of no benefit or impediment.

Evolution

In 2011 the California Academy of Science estimated that there are eight million, seven hundred thousand species of life on earth. This does not include millions of different bacteria and viruses. Evolutionists believe that lightening strikes on earth and water created proteins that came alive, then mutate into the enormous variety and uniqueness of earth's species. Scientists have been trying for years to replicate the process and have never produced a single living cell.

The Biblical statement that God "spoke" the earth's nine million life forms into existence may be hard to believe but current beliefs about evolution are no more credible. In the Bible God states that each species will reproduce in accordance with "its kind." Evolution research has shown that no new species has ever mutated into or been bred from an existing species. Evolution lab results support creation theory rather than evolution.

Getting Ready For Heaven

The Bible says (2 Corinthians 4:18) that what is unseen, the supernatural, is eternal but what is seen, worldliness, is temporary. Earthly death and leaving your body can occur at any age, so the vigilance I propose for my older friends is just as pertinent for the young. It just seems more pressing if you are old, using a cane, have a pacemaker and defibrillator implanted and your friends are dying!

So if you agree when people die they leave their body and go somewhere, and you concede there is intelligent design, then what is the next step when all your life you have denied the supernatural, and have an aversion for what you know about organized religion? Science offers no hope for understanding the supernatural. Studying the various religions for an answer is a reasonable approach. If your's is a late-in-life study, it is doubtful you will have enough time. I have been doing this for over thirty years and have come to a comfortable solution. God only knows how helpful it will be be to share my experience with you.

In Luke16:19-31, Jesus tells a parable to the religious but godless Pharisees that the nature of eternal life after death will be determined from what you believed and how you lived your life on earth. In other words, if you are going to get into Heaven, it has to be arranged *before* you die. Being a successful person on earth is not what opens the door into Heaven. A "Savior" is required. Too much self-confidence and self-reliance are handicaps for feeling this "need."

It has been hard for me to believe there was such a thing as Hell. If there was a Heaven, I had always assumed that a loving God would take me in. These old ways of thinking changed after reading the Bible. I learned there are answers for questions about

God, creation, death, and afterlife. To my consternation, the Bible said that going into Heaven is not automatic.

Is Jesus God?

A very important question because, like it or not, the Bible says an essential requirement for admission to Heaven is believing in Jesus.

There is little argument that Jesus was a man who literally walked on earth 2000 years ago. The question is whether he was God, a prophet, or a great teacher. Christians believe He was God who came to earth in the human form of Jesus Christ. Old Testament prophets, 500 to 2000 years before Jesus was born, predicted his birth. Prophesies included His being born of a virgin in Bethlehem, entering Jerusalem in triumph on a donkey, being betrayed by his own people, remaining silent before his accusers, dying by crucifixion, and being raised from the dead.

Matthew, Mark, Luke, and John, the four authors who described Jesus' life in the New Testament, were known as honest, mentally stable men. Their descriptions of Jesus' life and miracles were consistent with one another. Over five hundred people reported they had seen Jesus risen from the dead. These witnesses had nothing to gain from false testimony. To the contrary, after Jesus had been put to death, the apostles were tortured and killed for refusing to recant that they had seen Him alive. These martyrs would not have chosen death unless they had seen and experienced the truth of their conviction.

Jesus was not just a "good teacher." He, Himself, said he was God. The life of Jesus is not a fairy tale. No human would make up a god like Jesus. Our human fantasies would not have us worshipping a man who was born into poverty, unattractive, and persecuted. An imagined god would not wash the feet of his subjects. He would not allow himself to be ridiculed, flogged, and crucified. That this story of Jesus has endured two thousand years of criticism and challenge speaks to its validity, and its divinity.

Is the Bible the Word of God?

Any supernatural belief system is difficult for earthlings to conceive. Christianity and the Bible are no exception. However, studying the major religions has shown me no supernatural belief system (religion) more plausible than Christianity.

God answers our questions in the Bible. In it He explains how we should live in harmony on earth and what is necessary to receive eternal life in Heaven. The Bible is a supernatural instrument. No other book is like it and this is why:

- Christianity has an "owner's manual," the Holy Bible.
- The Bible is a single reference. All its instructions are in this one book.
- The Bible has remained current for 3000 years.
- The Bible is applicable to all cultures.
- The themes of the Bible in all of its 66 books are consistent even though the Bible was written over a period of 3000 years by 40 different authors who:
  1. had no copying machines
  2. had no computers
  3. had no phones,
  4. spoke different languages
  5. lived in different countries and continents
  6. had no knowledge of what others had written
- No archeological findings have refuted Biblical history.
- Prophesy in the Bible has been documented as true.
- Historically, most nations that practice Bible teaching prosper.
- Historically, most nations that abandon Biblical teaching collapse.
- The Bible is the most read book ever written. For me the most convincing evidence for the Bible being the inerrant Word of God is what happens in our weekly Bible Study. Each week forty to fifty worldly, intelligent, successful, men study and discuss the Bible. They find that the Bible's words written 3,000 years ago edify and enhance their modern lives more than any other resource. It demonstrates for me that although the words were written by men, their inspiration came from God.

When Reading The Bible Doesn't Help

Some of my friends who have earnestly tried to read the Bible and expose themselves to its wisdom and direction say it just doesn't come to them. Saying a silent prayer to access the Holy Spirit may solve this problem; a variation of something like this: *"God, I am not a Christian so I am not good at this. I have been told that if I ask you to direct my understanding I will get more out of reading the Bible. Please help me. Amen.*

The Bible says, John 14:26, that after Jesus rose into Heaven, God sent the Holy Spirit to remain on earth to expand on all the things Jesus had said. Saying such a prayer may be the first crack in our resistance to accept there is a higher power in control of our lives. It can be the forerunner of future communication with God through prayer.

The Bible is a supernatural phenomena. It is the Word of God. Reading it can change your life more than can be explained from just its intellectual instruction.

Another phenomena that complicates Biblical understanding is the reader becoming preoccupied with *why* God would say or do certain things. This is a futile task as no human is able to comprehend God's reasoning. The focus for the reader should be instead on what God is telling the reader *to do*. This will still leave plenty of room for interpretation and wonder. The Holy Spirit will direct you if you ask. Some statements in the Bible may have been intended primarily for another culture or individual. The Bible is inerrant. God did not mistakenly leave something in it. This does not mean that every word should be understood literally. The Bible should be interpreted with the help of the Holy Spirit and by discussion with other Christians. This is one way the Bible remains culturally and chronologically relevant. Bible Study groups are a great assist.

When Christianity Doesn't Seem Fair:

Some people refuse to accept the Bible because they cannot believe in a God who would only let people who believe in Jesus into Heaven. They think this is arbitrary, unfair, unreasonable, and unbelievable. They say they know people who are better and kinder than many Christians; therefore why should these people be denied heaven?

God makes the natural laws of the universe and earth so we can also assume there will be rules in Heaven. Heaven is said to be peaceful, with no illness, no sadness, no conflict, no crime or sin. Heaven will be unlike earth and that's a good thing. It figures that some rules will be different from the ones on earth. If we are going to get into a heavenly paradise we will have to fit in. To join God's family in Heaven we will have to be perfect like God.

Although there are many good people on earth, even the best person is not perfect. The only way for a human to get into Heaven is by way of a miracle. This is the supernatural phenomena that is described in the Bible. God sent his Son, Jesus, to take the punishment that would be enough to cancel our sin and make us perfect in order to live with God in Heaven.

Like gravity on earth, justice in Heaven is irrevocable. Justice is when people get what they deserve. That may not be a good thing. Justice demands that sin be punished. What most of us have in mind is "mercy."

"Justice" is when we get what we deserve.

"Mercy" is when we don't get what we deserve.

The best one, "Grace," is when we get what we don't deserve.

Jesus can give us grace but not unless we know about Him and ask Him for it. To receive grace all we have to do is ask for it in prayer.

This seems an unbelievably mild condition, considering what Christ took on in suffering for us on earth. We are told we will understand all this when we get to Heaven. Until then we have to accept this on faith. My recommendation is just accept it! Postpone understanding "why" until you get to Heaven. It probably is coming sooner than you have in mind.

When Pride Gets In The Way

Several of my friends have identified "pride" as their stumbling block to Christianity. Doctors are prone to cherish their knowledge of science to a degree that stubborn pride develops. This pride inhibits them from considering concepts that from their perspective do not meet scientific standards.

Considering the dire consequences, I suggest you swallow your pride, say a silent prayer, and begin to read the first four books of the New Testament of the Bible. This is only 146 pages and contains almost everything in the Bible that Christ did or said when he was on earth.

Remember, every Bible reading session must be preceded by a silent prayer asking that God (the Holy Spirit) open your mind to its wisdom. Without the prayer, it is not a fair test. Think of it being like a password required for opening a program on your computer or phone. You can not arbitrarily decide you will not use the password. You should not arbitrarily decide the silent prayer is unnecessary.

Unfair Death and Suffering

This is another of the Bibles mysteries that we will understand in our afterlife. *(Romans 8:28)* "And we know that for those who love God all things work together for good, for those who are called according to his purpose." The following are some points to consider:

- God must see some usefulness for suffering as he allowed his son, Jesus, to suffer greatly.
- If Heaven is so superior to earth, and time on earth is so short compared to time in Heaven, the suffering on earth may not be as consequential as we perceive. *(Romans 8:18)* "For I consider that the sufferings of this present time are not worth comparing with the glory that is to be revealed to us"
- The Bible says that there will be special rewards in heaven for humans who get shortchanged on earth. *(Mark 10:31)* "But many who are first will be last, and the last will be first."
- Suffering may bring a person to recognize the need for God.

- Suffering may build strengths needed for future adversity. *(James 1:12)* "Blessed is the man who remains steadfast under trial, for when he has stood the test he will receive the crown of life, which God has promised to those who love him"
- Could God allow early death because?
  - God has a special need for someone in Heaven?
  - A person has reached maximum benefit from earth life?
  - God perceives a person will suffer greatly on earth in the future?
  - A person's death will bring others to Christ?

Who knows? We will find out soon enough. In the meantime I am doing what I can to follow the steps an All-powerful God has provided in the Bible.

To deny God for what you consider to be unjust requirements for Heaven seems like jumping off a tall building because you don't agree with His position on gravity.

Emergency Salvation

Praying silently words like those below immediately provides "eternal-life insurance:"

Heavenly Father,
I confess that I am a sinner. I know there is no way I can undo my sinfulness through my own efforts.
I understand that Jesus Christ came to earth, suffered, and died to pay for my sin.
I acknowledge Jesus as my Lord and Savior.
I accept His grace and His gift of eternal life.
Amen

This is something that should be done "stat." It is a golden parachute that the Bible says will get you through the gate into Heaven. John 3:16 "For God so loved the world, that He gave His only begotten Son, that whoever believes in Him shall not perish, but have eternal life." Don't wait for more information. If you, like the criminal on the cross next to Jesus, died soon after accepting Christ as Savior, it would be good timing but I wouldn't count on it.

Living A Christian Life

Assuming you don't drop dead after saying the prayer above you will discover there is much more to living a Christian life than saying the simple prayer and reading the Bible. Our salvation is God's gift; the sign of acceptance of this gift is living a Christian life.

Weight Watchers and Alcoholics' Anonymous only benefits those who attend their meetings; it is not enough to just read their literature. If you think it is difficult to lose weight or stop drinking, try on your own to live a life without sin. Associating with other Christians by attending a church is recommended.

When humans accept the grace of Jesus Christ, the Holy Spirit empowers them to change. People notice they are different. They see these new Christians developing "fruit of the Spirit (Galatians 5:22-23)." The Bible says these are love, joy, peace, patience, kindness, goodness, faithfulness, gentleness and self-control.

Alcohol

There is one aspect of Godlessness that demands further discussion as a warning to others in my family. Although Jesus' first miracle was turning water into wine, He also urges moderation. Moderation is not a Myers family characteristic. Our bloodline has a history of alcohol use to a degree that behavior and personal relationships are compromised. Many of our relatives could be considered alcoholics.

Alcohol has been a temptation and problem for me. It is only through the grace of God that my alcohol history has not been more destructive. Severe hangovers have been a blessing as they limit the times that I drink. Most of the times when I have done things of which I am ashamed have been when drinking.

Controlling drinking has taken energy that could have been used much more productively. Be forewarned. Your financial success, your marriage, your relationships with friends, your faith, your health, and the way that you will age will be adversely effected if you drink to excess. It may be possible to continue to drink with our genetic pattern but the energy to control it over a life time may not be worth it. It is a lot easier to make that decision now than to be forced into it after you are a recognized drunk.

Should you **decide to quit drinking**, there is one thing certain, **it won't hurt you!**

P.S. You don't want to, even as a joke, receive a letter like the one I received, shown on the next page.

THE REVEREND ELTON "SALVATION" JONES
THE RESCUE MISSION
1529 SAVIOR AVENUE
SWEETWATER, TEXAS 76067

Dan A. Myers, M.D.
5110 Tracy
Dallas, Texas 75205

Dear Dan:

Perhaps you have heard of me and my nationwide campaign in the cause of temperance. Each year for the past fourteen years, I have made a tour of Arkansas, Louisiana, Texas, Mississippi and Alabama delivering a series of lectures on the evils of drinking. On this tour I have been accompanied by my young friend and assistant, Clyde Linsom. Clyde, a young man of good family and excellent background, is a pathetic example of life ruined by excessive indulgence in whiskey and women.

Clyde would appear with me at lectures and sit on the platform drunk, wheezing, staring at the audience through bloodshot and bleary eyes, sweating profusely, picking at his nose, passing gas, and making obscene gestures while I would point out him as an example of what overindulgence can do to a person.

This winter, unfortunately, Clyde died. A mutual friend has given us your name, and I wonder if you would be available to take Clyde's place on my next tour?

Yours in faith,

Elton

Reverend Elton "Salvation" Jones
Rescue Mission

The Bottom Line

Nothing beats living a Christian life with the hope of eternal bliss in Heaven. Thank God I have lived long enough to understand that no matter how self-reliant one seems, God continues to be in control of our destiny.

I pray someone will learn from my experience. God Bless You. I hope to see you in Heaven.

Dan and Kathy Myers

Reading Suggestions

The Life Application Study Bible, New Living Translation, Tyndale House Publishers – This Bible is written in everyday English and contains footnotes, maps, and timelines that make it interesting and understandable. If you have never read the Bible, I suggest you begin at "Matthew," the first book of the New Testament.

Darwin On Trial, by Phillip Johnson tells how Darwinism has become so accepted as "fact" that it is not held to modern scientific standards. Dr. Jones reviews scientific research to show that popular views about evolution are more similar to "faith" than science.

The Battle For The Beginning, Creation, Evolution, and the Bible by John MacArthur, one of the nations foremost Bible teachers, will shock you as he clearly explains how we have been beguiled and bullied into accepting that evolution is scientifically supported.

The Jesus I Never Knew, Phillip Yansey – Dr. Billy Graham described Phillip Yancey as, "the modern writer who I most admire." The Jesus I Never Knew explains the Christian faith in a way that leaves one thinking, "Why hasn't someone told me that way before?"

More than A Carpenter, by Josh Mc Dowell. A down to earth book that explains the basics of the Christian faith. Millions of books in print.

Jesus On Trial, by David Limbaugh is a very thorough testimony of a lawyer to the validity and truth of the Bible.

Know Why You Believe, Paul E. Little, InterVarsity Press, Downers Grove, Illinois. – A short, easy to read book that answers most challenges to a Christian faith. Mr. Little's responses are logical, compelling, and enlightening.

<u>Mere Christianity</u>, C.S. Lewis, C.S. Lewis, the author of Tales of Narnia, is an extraordinary storyteller and a distinguished scholar. How this brilliant atheist became a devout Christian, is logically and engagingly
presented.

<u>One Minute After You Die</u>, Erwin W. Lutzer, this small booklet heavily uses references from the Bible to paint a picture of what can be expected when one dies. The result may scare the pants off of you.

<u>The Purpose Driven Life</u>, Rick Warren, Explains passionately how important it is for us to understand that we are only passing through this world preparing for eternal life in Heaven.

www.ingramcontent.com/pod-product-compliance
Lightning Source LLC
Chambersburg PA
CBHW060833110426
R18122100001BA/R181221PG42736CBX00017BA/7